Uncover Your Extra Income Potential.
Discover, Decide, and Do!

WAYS TO MAKE EXTRA INCOME

Ways To Make Extra Income provides a comprehensive guide to various online earning opportunities, including real estate, writing, art, product sales, and more, to help readers explore diverse options for boosting their income.

Vanessa Han

Ways To Make Extra Income

Introduction: The Importance of Diversifying Income Streams

Understanding Income Diversification

In today's rapidly changing economic landscape, individuals are increasingly recognizing the value of diversifying their income streams as a means of bolstering their financial security. The concept of income diversification entails the allocation of resources across a variety of sources, such as investments, side businesses, and passive income avenues, rather than relying solely on a single source of income. This approach serves as a proactive strategy to mitigate the risks associated with relying on a singular income source, which can leave individuals vulnerable to unforeseen economic downturns or industry-specific challenges.

The significance of income diversification becomes particularly evident in times of economic uncertainty, where traditional employment models may prove unpredictable or unstable. By cultivating multiple streams of income, individuals can enhance their economic resilience and adaptability, thereby fostering greater stability and autonomy in navigating financial fluctuations. Embracing income diversification also empowers individuals to pursue opportunities that align with their passions and expertise, leading to a more fulfilling and dynamic professional journey.

The benefits of income diversification extend beyond financial fortification, encompassing broader personal and professional growth. Through the pursuit of varied income streams, individuals are encouraged to expand their skill sets, explore new industries, and cultivate an entrepreneurial mindset. This multifaceted approach to income generation not only fosters a diversified financial portfolio but also nurtures creativity, resourcefulness, and adaptability, essential qualities in an increasingly competitive and dynamic global economy.

Furthermore, by diversifying their income, individuals position themselves to capitalize on evolving market trends, emerging technologies, and shifting consumer behaviors. This adaptive capacity enables them to stay ahead of the curve, harnessing new opportunities for financial gain and professional fulfillment. In an age defined by rapid technological advancements and interconnected global markets, the ability to pivot and innovate within various income-generating endeavors is instrumental for long-term success and relevance.

As we delve deeper into the intricacies of income diversification, it becomes evident that this multifaceted approach embodies a philosophy of proactive wealth creation and risk management. As individuals engage with the diverse pathways of income diversification, they are poised to not only safeguard their financial well-being but also unlock a world of possibilities, from pursuing entrepreneurial ventures to achieving a balanced lifestyle that harmonizes work and personal pursuits.

Economic Resilience Through Multiple Streams

Economic resilience refers to the ability of individuals and households to withstand financial shocks and navigate through uncertain economic conditions. One key strategy for enhancing economic resilience is the pursuit of multiple income streams. By diversifying sources of income, individuals can mitigate the impact of potential disruptions in any one particular sector or market, thus bolstering their overall financial stability. This approach not only provides a safety net during challenging times but also offers the potential for increased wealth accumulation and economic empowerment.

Diversifying income streams can significantly reduce vulnerability to economic downturns, job insecurities, and unforeseen expenses. For instance, an individual who solely relies on a single source of income, such as employment, faces heightened risk in instances of industry layoffs, company downsizing, or unexpected medical expenses. Having supplementary streams of income from investments, freelance work, or side projects can serve as a reliable cushion during such adversities, ensuring continued financial sustainability. In this way, the diversification of income acts as a shield, fortifying against the uncertainties perpetually looming in today's dynamic economic landscape.

Furthermore, adopting a multi-pronged income approach fosters a mindset of proactive financial planning and resourcefulness. It encourages individuals to explore and leverage their skills, knowledge, and interests to create value in alternative arenas, thereby broadening their horizons and opening up new avenues for prosperity. With diverse income sources, individuals are also better positioned to capitalize on emerging opportunities and trends in various sectors, harnessing the potential for greater financial rewards and stability.

Beyond individuals, communities and societies at large also stand to benefit from the cultivation of multiple income streams. A populace with diversified economic resources is more resilient and less susceptible to widespread financial crises, which can have cascading effects on social well-being and stability. As such, advocating for the adoption of a diversified income mindset contributes to the overall economic vitality and sustainability of entire regions and nations.

In summary, honing a portfolio of multiple income streams not only offers a buffer against financial hardships but also paves the way for enhanced wealth-building and economic adaptability. This chapter has underscored the critical link between economic resilience and the diversification of income, laying a foundation for the subsequent exploration of strategies and approaches to cultivate and maximize diversified earnings.

The Global Perspective on Diversified Earnings

In today's interconnected and rapidly evolving global economy, the concept of diversified earnings has transcended geographical boundaries to become a fundamental aspect of financial stability and growth. Across the world, individuals and businesses are increasingly recognizing the importance of creating multiple streams of income to navigate economic uncertainties, seize opportunities, and build resilient financial portfolios. This shift in mindset is driven by the realization that relying on a single source of income is inherently vulnerable to external shocks, market fluctuations, and industry-specific challenges. Embracing a diversified approach to earnings provides a safety net and enables individuals to adapt to changing circumstances with greater agility. From emerging economies to developed nations, the pursuit of diversified earnings reflects a universal aspiration for security, prosperity, and autonomy. In many regions, this trend is further amplified by the rising prevalence of remote work, freelancing, and digital entrepreneurship, which has empowered individuals to explore diverse income-generating avenues without traditional constraints. The global perspective on diversified earnings also underscores a crucial aspect of financial inclusivity and empowerment. By promoting the diversification of income streams, societies can mitigate socioeconomic disparities, foster entrepreneurship, and create pathways for economic advancement among diverse populations. Moreover, the emphasis on diversified earnings resonates deeply with the principles of sustainability and adaptability in an era characterized by rapid technological innovation and shifting market dynamics. As the traditional boundaries of employment and commerce continue to blur, individuals and organizations are redefining conventional notions of work and income generation. This evolving landscape demands a comprehensive understanding of the diverse cultural, regulatory, and economic contexts in which diversified earnings operate worldwide. Moreover, cross-cultural insights offer valuable lessons and inspiration, illuminating innovative approaches and success stories that transcend borders. Understanding the global dynamics of diversified earnings equips individuals with a holistic perspective that transcends parochial limitations, enriches strategic decision-making, and fosters a spirit of collaboration and exchange. By venturing beyond traditional models and embracing a culturally informed approach to income diversification, individuals can leverage unique opportunities, adapt best practices, and cultivate a broadened outlook that elevates their financial prospects and resilience in a complex, interconnected world.

Assessing Risk Management Strategies

Whenever embarking on the journey of income diversification, it is essential to recognize and evaluate the associated risks. While diversifying income streams can offer numerous benefits, it is not without pitfalls. The prudent management of these risks is crucial to ensuring long-term financial stability. In this section, we will delve into an in-depth exploration of various risk management strategies that can be employed to mitigate potential challenges.

One fundamental risk to consider is the possibility of overextending oneself. Diversifying income streams requires time, effort, and resources, and spreading too thin across different ventures may result in subpar performance in all areas. It is important to carefully assess one's capacity and capabilities before venturing into new income avenues. Additionally, understanding the inherent volatility of certain income sources, such as stock market investments or freelance work, is paramount. By conducting thorough research and seeking expert advice, individuals can equip themselves with the knowledge needed to make informed decisions about their income diversification journey.

Another critical aspect of risk management is the implementation of a robust financial plan. Effective budgeting, prudent savings habits, and a well-defined emergency fund are key components of a sound financial strategy. By establishing a financial safety net, individuals can mitigate the impact of unforeseen economic downturns, sudden expenses, or business setbacks. Moreover, consider the acquisition of insurance coverage tailored to protect against specific risks associated with diverse income streams, such as liability insurance for freelance consultants or rental property insurance for real estate investors.

Furthermore, when evaluating potential income opportunities, it is imperative to conduct comprehensive risk assessments for each venture. This involves analyzing market trends, competitive landscapes, and potential regulatory changes that could impact the profitability of the endeavor. Initiating a scenario analysis to gauge the best- and worst-case outcomes allows for informed decision-making and proactive risk mitigation. Conducting sensitivity analyses to evaluate the impact of external variables, such as interest rate fluctuations or commodity price shifts, can aid in the identification of potential vulnerabilities.

Additionally, it is essential to address the digital risks associated with modern income diversification. As technological advancements continue to shape the global economy, individuals must remain vigilant against cybersecurity threats, data breaches, and online fraud. Implementing robust cybersecurity measures, utilizing secure payment gateways, and staying informed about emerging cyber threats are indispensable in safeguarding the financial integrity of digital income streams.

Ultimately, successful income diversification hinges on the ability to identify and assess risks proactively. Employing a multifaceted risk management approach, grounded in prudence and foresight, can safeguard one's financial well-being and pave the way for sustained prosperity.

Case Studies: Success Stories of Income Diversification

In examining the concept of income diversification, it is invaluable to delve into real-life examples of individuals and businesses that have successfully implemented diversified income strategies. These case studies serve as compelling illustrations of the potential benefits and challenges associated with pursuing multiple streams of income.

One noteworthy case study centers on a freelance writer who expanded her portfolio beyond traditional journalism to encompass content creation for digital marketing agencies, ghostwriting books, and developing online courses. By diversifying her writing services, she not only multiplied her revenue streams but also gained exposure to a broader clientele, thereby enhancing her professional network and industry expertise. This case demonstrates the capacity of diversification to elevate skill sets and increase marketability.

Similarly, a real estate investor's journey provides insight into the advantages of income diversification within the property sector. Upon recognizing the volatility inherent in real estate markets, this investor diversified by acquiring rental properties in addition to actively participating in real estate crowdfunding platforms. Consequently, during periods of market fluctuation, rental income offered stability while crowdfunding contributed to portfolio growth. These varied investments ultimately mitigated risk and bolstered the investor's financial resilience.

Another compelling case study unfolds in the realm of ecommerce, where an independent artisan leveraged various online platforms to expand her customer base. While initially reliant on a single marketplace, she recognized the vulnerability of such dependence and diversified by establishing her e-commerce website, leveraging social media for direct sales, and participating in artisan markets. Through these diverse channels, she cultivated a loyal customer following and insulated her business from the potential impact of any platform changes or disruptions.

Furthermore, the story of a software developer underscores the significance of diversifying income within the tech industry. Beyond his primary software development role, this individual engaged in freelance coding projects, provided technical consultations, and developed and licensed proprietary plugins. As a result, he not only amplified his earnings but also broadened his proficiencies and created a safety net against fluctuations in project demands and industry trends.

These case studies collectively underscore the transformative potential of income diversification in fostering financial security, empowering professional development, and fortifying resilience amid economic uncertainties. By exploring and internalizing these success stories, readers can gain valuable insights and inspiration to embark on their own income diversification journeys.

Financial Security: Preparing for Uncertainty

In an ever-evolving economic landscape, ensuring financial security is paramount in navigating the uncertainties of the future. As the world witnesses rapid technological advancements and unpredictable global events, individuals are compelled to fortify their financial position through strategic planning and proactive measures. Achieving financial security involves not only optimizing existing income streams but also diversifying earnings to mitigate potential risks. A balanced combination of regular income, passive investments, and alternative revenue sources can create a safety net against unforeseen challenges. Furthermore, developing a robust emergency fund alongside prudent budgeting can safeguard against abrupt financial disruptions, reinforcing overall stability. Planning for retirement and long-term financial goals is essential in securing a lasting safety net. By investing in retirement accounts, pension plans, and other investment vehicles early on, individuals can ensure financial independence during their later years. The cultivation of multiple income streams presents a pivotal strategy in achieving financial security. Beyond traditional employment, exploring opportunities in real estate, stock market investments, freelancing, and entrepreneurship can bolster financial resilience. Effective asset allocation is equally imperative in building a diverse investment portfolio, spreading risk across various asset classes and industries. Embracing the role of technology can also enhance financial security, as digital platforms offer avenues for remote work, online business ventures, and investment management. Additionally, staying informed about financial trends and leveraging professional advice can further equip individuals with the necessary tools to navigate complex financial landscapes. Understanding market dynamics, investment instruments, and potential shifts in economic paradigms empowers individuals to adapt proactively, thereby safeguarding their financial well-being. To reinforce financial security, it is imperative to cultivate a mindset of continual learning and adaptability. Adopting resilient financial habits, coupled with ongoing education in financial planning and management, can fortify an individual's readiness to face uncertainties. Undertaking periodic reassessments of financial goals and adjusting strategies in response to changing circumstances ensures alignment with evolving financial objectives. Ultimately, prioritizing financial security is an ongoing journey that demands vigilance, prudence, and resourcefulness. By employing a multifaceted approach encompassing diversified income streams, adaptive investment strategies, and disciplined financial planning, individuals can fortify their resilience against financial uncertainty, thereby nurturing enduring financial security.

Identifying Potential Income Opportunities

To identify potential income opportunities, individuals need to assess their skills, expertise, and market demand. This process involves comprehensive self-reflection to determine what unique value proposition one can offer. It's crucial to leverage strengths and passions while considering market trends and consumer needs. One approach is conducting a SWOT analysis (Strengths, Weaknesses, Opportunities, Threats) to gain insights into personal capabilities and external factors that may impact income ventures.

Additionally, exploring emerging industries and gaps in existing markets can unveil promising prospects. Researching industries on the cusp of growth or undergoing significant transformations can uncover fertile ground for income diversification. From renewable energy to digital marketing, staying informed about market dynamics is key.

Furthermore, networking with professionals across diverse fields can provide valuable exposure to potential income-generating activities. Attending industry events, engaging in online forums, and seeking mentorship can lead to meaningful connections and newfound opportunities. Collaborating with like-minded individuals often leads to innovative income streams and partnerships.

Moreover, honing in on emerging technological advancements offers enormous potential. Embracing automation, artificial intelligence, and other disruptive technologies can open doors to novel income avenues. For instance, leveraging social media platforms, creating online courses, or providing freelance services in high-demand programming languages can yield substantial returns.

It's essential to remain adaptable and responsive to market shifts when evaluating income prospects. The gig economy, remote work opportunities, and the rise of e-commerce present evolving income landscapes. Recognizing these shifts and adapting skill sets accordingly can position individuals ahead of the curve.

Diversifying income through portfolio investments, royalties, and passive income streams should also be explored. Real estate, stocks, bonds, and intellectual property can offer financial resilience and long-term stability. Additionally, understanding taxation laws and financial planning is vital to optimize income diversification strategies.

Conclusively, identifying potential income opportunities demands a proactive, multidimensional approach. By synergizing personal talents, embracing technology, staying abreast of industry trends, and capitalizing on evolving economic landscapes, individuals can unlock a multitude of income pathways.

The Role of Technology in Diversifying Income

In today's rapidly evolving digital landscape, technology plays a pivotal role in enabling individuals to diversify their income streams. The advent of the internet and various technological advancements has significantly transformed the way people can generate revenue. One of the primary ways technology facilitates income diversification is through the creation of online platforms and marketplaces. These platforms provide individuals with the opportunity to showcase their skills, products, or services to a global audience, thereby expanding their potential customer base and earning opportunities.

Furthermore, technology has revolutionized the concept of remote work, allowing individuals to engage in various income-generating activities without geographical constraints. The rise of freelancing, online consulting, and digital product sales has been made possible by advancements in communication technology and collaboration tools. This flexibility in work arrangements empowers individuals to pursue diverse income avenues while maintaining a balanced lifestyle.

Moreover, the integration of automation and artificial intelligence (AI) has streamlined numerous business processes, making it more efficient for entrepreneurs to manage multiple income streams simultaneously. Automated marketing tools, data analytics platforms, and e-commerce solutions have made it easier than ever for individuals to establish and scale their ventures with minimal manual intervention, thus enabling them to focus on creating additional revenue sources.

Additionally, the emergence of blockchain technology and cryptocurrency has opened up new possibilities for income diversification. Individuals can now participate in decentralized finance (DeFi), invest in digital assets, and explore innovative funding mechanisms such as initial coin offerings (ICOs) and tokenization. These developments illustrate how technology continues to reshape traditional financial systems, offering alternative paths for individuals to bolster their income portfolios.

It is imperative for individuals seeking to diversify their income to embrace technological advancements and continually adapt to emerging trends. Staying informed about new platforms, tools, and market opportunities will be essential for capitalizing on the potential that technology offers for income diversification. However, it is also crucial to approach technology with a discerning eye, as the landscape is constantly evolving, and not all tech-based income opportunities may align with one's long-term goals and risk tolerance.

In conclusion, technology serves as a catalyst for income diversification, providing individuals with unprecedented access to varied revenue streams and empowering them to leverage their skills and resources in innovative ways. Embracing technology as a tool for income diversification requires a proactive approach, ongoing learning, and strategic decision-making to maximize its potential benefits while navigating associated risks.

Overcoming Common Challenges

As individuals venture into diversifying their income streams, they are likely to encounter a range of challenges that can impede their progress. In this section, we will explore some of the most prevalent obstacles and provide actionable strategies for overcoming them. One common challenge faced by many is the fear of failure and the associated risk aversion. Diversifying income often involves stepping out of one's comfort zone and embracing new opportunities, which can be daunting for some. However, by reframing failure as a learning experience and recognizing that a diversified portfolio can mitigate risks, individuals can gain the confidence needed to pursue new income avenues. Another challenge is the lack of time and resources to effectively manage multiple income streams. Balancing various sources of income alongside personal and professional commitments can be overwhelming. To address this, it is essential to prioritize tasks, delegate responsibilities where possible, and leverage technology and automation to streamline processes. Moreover, setting realistic goals and timelines can help individuals manage their time more efficiently and avoid burnout. Additionally, navigating the legal and financial complexities of diverse income streams can pose a significant challenge. Tax implications, legal regulations, and financial management differ across various sources of income, demanding a thorough understanding of these aspects. Seeking professional guidance from accountants, legal advisors, and financial experts is crucial in effectively managing these complexities. Furthermore, establishing robust record-keeping practices and maintaining clear documentation can aid in ensuring compliance and mitigating potential risks. Amidst the challenges, the need for adaptability and resilience becomes paramount. Economic conditions, market trends, and consumer behaviors are constantly evolving, presenting continual challenges for individuals with diversified income streams. Flexibility and the ability to pivot in response to changing circumstances are essential attributes for success in this landscape. Embracing a growth mindset, staying informed about industry developments, and remaining open to innovation are fundamental in overcoming these dynamic challenges. Lastly, finding a balance between specialization and diversification can be a daunting task. While diversifying income is advantageous, spreading oneself too thin across disparate ventures can dilute focus and effectiveness. Striking a balance between exploring new opportunities and honing existing skills is crucial. Through strategic planning, individuals can identify complementary income streams that align with their expertise while broadening their financial portfolio. By proactively addressing these common challenges, individuals can fortify their journey toward diversifying income and position themselves for long-term success.

Setting Strong Foundations for Future Chapters

Now that we have explored the myriad challenges associated with diversifying income streams, it is imperative to establish a framework that will underpin and guide our journey through the subsequent chapters. Setting strong foundations is the key to unlocking the potential of any endeavor, and the pursuit of diversified income is no exception.

First and foremost, it is essential to cultivate a mindset that embraces adaptability and continuous learning. As we navigate through various income-generating avenues, being open to new ideas, strategies, and methodologies will be crucial in shaping our success. Furthermore, fostering a proactive attitude towards change and innovation will empower us to stay ahead of market trends and consumer demands.

In addition to a flexible mindset, establishing clear objectives and goals for each income stream is fundamental. By delineating specific targets and benchmarks, we can effectively measure our progress and identify areas for improvement. This strategic approach will also enable us to allocate resources efficiently and prioritize activities that align with our overarching financial aspirations.

Furthermore, as we embark on this journey, creating a robust support network will be vital in providing guidance, encouragement, and insights. Surrounding ourselves with like-minded individuals who share our ambition for diversified earnings can offer valuable mentorship opportunities and collaborative partnerships. Leveraging the expertise and experiences of others within our network can provide invaluable lessons and shortcuts to success.

Moreover, laying the groundwork for future chapters involves adopting a disciplined approach to managing time and resources. Effectively balancing our commitments, prioritizing tasks, and optimizing productivity will be critical in ensuring that each income stream receives the attention and effort it deserves. Implementing efficient systems and processes to streamline workflows and minimize distractions will facilitate sustainable growth across multiple ventures.

Lastly, acknowledging and mitigating the risks associated with venturing into diverse income sources is instrumental in setting enduring foundations. By conducting thorough risk assessments, implementing contingency plans, and continuously monitoring market dynamics, we can proactively safeguard our financial endeavors from unforeseen disruptions.

By embracing these foundational principles, we lay the groundwork for an enriching and rewarding exploration of diversified income streams in the forthcoming chapters.

Ways To Make Extra Income

Real Estate Investments: Building Wealth with Property

Understanding the Real Estate Market Landscape

In order to make informed decisions and navigate the dynamic real estate market, it is imperative for investors to gain a comprehensive understanding of the current market landscape. This entails conducting thorough research to evaluate prevailing trends, both at a macroeconomic level and specific to individual regions or cities. By analyzing market trends, investors can identify opportune periods for investment, taking advantage of fluctuations and predicting potential future growth.

Furthermore, regional developments play a pivotal role in influencing property values. Factors such as urbanization, infrastructure projects, and demographic shifts can significantly impact the desirability and value of real estate in a given area. Moreover, staying abreast of regulatory changes and economic indicators is essential to gauge the health and direction of the real estate market.

By comprehensively assessing the real estate market landscape, investors can position themselves strategically, identifying promising investment opportunities while mitigating potential risks. An in-depth understanding of market dynamics empowers investors to make well-informed decisions, ultimately maximizing the potential for long-term wealth creation.

Types of Real Estate Investments

Real estate investment offers diverse options for individuals seeking to build wealth through property. Understanding the different types of real estate investments is crucial for making informed decisions in this lucrative market. One common avenue for investment is residential properties, encompassing single-family homes, condominiums, townhouses, and multifamily dwellings. Residential properties appeal to investors due to their potential for steady rental income and long-term appreciation. Commercial real estate presents another significant opportunity, including office buildings, retail spaces, industrial properties, and hospitality establishments such as hotels and resorts. Investing in commercial properties can yield substantial returns, with lease agreements often structured to provide stable income streams. Additionally, investors can explore the realm of industrial real estate, which includes warehouses, distribution centers, and manufacturing facilities. The industrial sector offers opportunities for investors to capitalize on the growing e-commerce and logistics industries. Another notable avenue for real estate investment is the realm of raw land and developmental properties. Investors can purchase undeveloped land or properties with potential for rezoning and development, aiming to capitalize on future appreciation and construction projects. Moreover, real estate investment trusts (REITs) enable investors to gain exposure to the real estate market without direct property ownership. REITs, which often specialize in specific property types such as residential, commercial, or healthcare properties, provide an avenue for passive income and portfolio diversification. Furthermore, real estate crowdfunding platforms have emerged as a modern method for investing in properties with lower capital requirements. Through crowdfunding, individuals can participate in real estate projects, ranging from residential developments to commercial ventures, alongside other investors. Understanding these varied types of real estate investments equips individuals with the knowledge needed to evaluate opportunities, mitigate risks, and make informed choices that align with their investment goals and risk tolerance.

Financing Your Property Investment

When delving into the world of real estate investment, one of the most crucial aspects to consider is the financing of your property ventures. Successful and profitable property investment often hinges on securing reliable and sustainable funding. As an investor, it is essential to explore and understand the various financing options available, as well as their implications and suitability for different types of real estate investments.

The process of financing a property investment typically involves a comprehensive assessment of personal or business financial capacity, creditworthiness, and overall market conditions. Traditional mortgage financing through banks or lending institutions is a common avenue for acquiring residential properties. This method often requires a substantial down payment and adherence to stringent approval criteria. On the other hand, commercial properties and larger investment opportunities may necessitate more complex financing structures, including commercial loans, private equity, or partnerships.

Moreover, alternative financing avenues such as hard money loans, real estate crowdfunding, and seller financing have gained popularity in recent years, providing investors with additional flexibility and creativity in structuring their property acquisitions. Understanding the advantages, risks, and terms associated with these alternative financing methods is crucial for making informed investment decisions.

While evaluating potential financing sources, it is imperative to conduct thorough due diligence and seek professional advice to ensure alignment with your investment goals, risk tolerance, and long-term strategy. Additionally, cultivating strong relationships with reputable lenders, financial advisors, and industry experts can provide valuable insights and access to favorable financing terms.

Furthermore, incorporating leverage as a strategic tool in property investment can amplify returns but also introduces inherent risks. Balancing the use of leverage with the potential benefits and risks is a fundamental consideration that necessitates a prudent and calculated approach. Understanding the intricacies of leveraging, loan terms, amortization schedules, and interest rates is essential for optimizing the financial structure of your real estate investments.

In conclusion, navigating the landscape of property investment financing requires a blend of financial acumen, market knowledge, and strategic foresight. By carefully assessing the available financing options, engaging in rigorous financial analysis, and seeking expert guidance, investors can position themselves for success in building wealth through property investments.

Evaluating Potential Properties: Key Metrics and Considerations

When evaluating potential properties for investment, it is crucial to consider a range of key metrics and factors to make informed decisions. The process begins with thorough market research to understand the local real estate landscape, including property values, rental rates, and neighborhood dynamics. This data provides valuable insights into the potential return on investment and long-term growth prospects. Moreover, analyzing market trends and economic indicators can help investors identify emerging opportunities and anticipate future demand. Additionally, assessing the property's location is paramount. Proximity to schools, amenities, public transportation, and employment centers is often indicative of a higher resale value and rental appeal.

Beyond location, the physical condition of the property is a critical consideration. Conducting a comprehensive inspection to evaluate the structural integrity, mechanical systems, and overall maintenance needs is essential. Engaging with qualified inspectors and contractors can provide a detailed understanding of any necessary repairs or renovations, enabling accurate budgeting and forecasting of expenses. Furthermore, zoning regulations, building codes, and potential development projects in the area should be thoroughly researched to ascertain any impacts on the property's value and future use.

Financial analysis forms a pivotal part of property evaluation. Calculating the potential return on investment through metrics such as cap rate, cash-on-cash return, and net operating income provides a quantitative basis for decision-making. Moreover, assessing the financing options available and understanding the implications of different loan structures, interest rates, and terms is crucial for optimizing the investment's financial performance. Additionally, evaluating the tax implications, including property taxes and potential incentives, assists in projecting the property's overall profitability.

Furthermore, considering the management aspects of the property is vital. For buy-and-hold investments, examining the potential challenges and costs associated with property management, tenant turnover, and ongoing maintenance is imperative to estimate the operational responsibilities and associated expenses. Finally, conducting a risk assessment by identifying potential market fluctuations, regulatory changes, and external factors that may impact the property's value and performance allows investors to develop risk mitigation strategies and contingency plans. Overall, incorporating these key metrics and considerations into the property evaluation process empowers investors to make informed decisions and build a robust real estate portfolio.

The Buy-and-Hold Strategy for Long-term Growth

Successful real estate investors often employ the buy-and-hold strategy as a cornerstone of their investment approach. This long-term wealth-building strategy involves acquiring properties with the intention of holding them for an extended period, typically in the range of five to ten years or even longer. The primary goal of the buy-and-hold strategy is to benefit from appreciation in property values over time, generating wealth through sustained growth and equity accumulation.

One of the fundamental advantages of the buy-and-hold strategy lies in its ability to leverage the power of compounding returns. By holding onto a property for the long term, investors can capitalize on the dual forces of property appreciation and mortgage equity buildup. As property values increase and the mortgage balance decreases, the investor's equity stake in the property grows, providing a source of passive wealth accumulation.

Furthermore, the buy-and-hold strategy offers the potential for consistent passive income through rental cash flows. By renting out the property to tenants, investors can generate regular monthly income while continuing to realize property appreciation over time. This dual-income stream bolsters the financial stability of the investment and further contributes to the long-term growth potential of the portfolio.

In addition to financial benefits, the buy-and-hold strategy also offers tax advantages, such as long-term capital gains treatment. When an investor holds a property for more than a year before selling, any profits from the sale may be subject to favorable long-term capital gains tax rates, providing potential tax savings compared to short-term investments. This tax advantage adds another layer of appeal to the buy-and-hold strategy, enhancing the overall returns on investment.

Implementing a successful buy-and-hold strategy requires meticulous property selection based on factors such as location, market trends, potential for value appreciation, and rental demand. Furthermore, investors must demonstrate a long-term mindset, as this strategy necessitates patience and a commitment to weathering market fluctuations and economic cycles. Additionally, diligent property management and maintenance are essential to preserving the asset's value and ensuring sustained long-term growth.

Ultimately, the buy-and-hold strategy represents a prudent and effective method for building enduring wealth through real estate investment. By harnessing the power of long-term property ownership, investors can capitalize on appreciation, generate consistent income, enjoy tax advantages, and fortify their financial outlook for the future.

Flipping Houses: Short-term Investment Opportunities

Flipping houses has long been an enticing avenue for short-term investment opportunities within the real estate market. This strategy involves purchasing a property, often one in need of renovation or repair, at a lower value, improving and updating it, then selling it at a higher price to yield a profitable return on investment (ROI). The key to successful house flipping lies in identifying properties with potential, accurately estimating renovation costs, and executing the necessary improvements within a specified timeframe. To excel in this domain, investors must possess a keen eye for spotting undervalued properties and understanding the local housing market trends and buyer preferences. Furthermore, adept project management skills are essential for overseeing the renovation process effectively and efficiently. Building a reliable network of contractors, suppliers, and real estate professionals can streamline the flipping process, ensuring quality workmanship and cost-effective solutions. Timing is critical in the house flipping business, as holding onto a property for too long can erode potential profits and increase financial risks. Therefore, meticulous planning and swift execution are paramount. Additionally, comprehensive market research and analysis are imperative for accurately projecting the resale value of the renovated property. Effective marketing strategies and staging techniques play a pivotal role in presenting the flipped property in an appealing light, thus maximizing its market appeal and sale potential. It is essential for house flippers to remain adaptable and responsive to unforeseen challenges, such as unexpected renovation costs or shifts in the local housing market. While flipping houses offers the allure of substantial financial gains, it also entails inherent risks, including the potential for overestimating the sale price or underestimating renovation expenses. Hence, thorough due diligence, prudent budgeting, and a contingency plan are fundamental safeguards against adverse outcomes. Successful house flipping demands a combination of industry knowledge, strategic vision, financial acumen, and perseverance. By embracing calculated risks and leveraging market insights, investors can harness the lucrative potential of flipping houses, creating valuable short-term investment opportunities within the dynamic real estate landscape.

Building a Diversified Real Estate Portfolio

Building a diversified real estate portfolio is essential for long-term success and stability in the world of property investment. While the concept of diversification is often associated with stock portfolios, it holds equal importance in the realm of real estate. Diversifying your real estate portfolio involves expanding your investments across different types of properties, locations, and investment strategies to mitigate risk and maximize returns. By spreading your investments across various property types, such as residential, commercial, and industrial, you can reduce the impact of market fluctuations on any single segment of your portfolio. Similarly, diversifying geographically across different regions or cities can help protect your portfolio from localized economic downturns or shifts in market demand. When considering investment strategies, mixing long-term buy-and-hold properties with shorter-term flipping opportunities can add balance and flexibility to your portfolio, catering to both steady income streams and potential windfall profits. Moreover, incorporating different financing structures, such as traditional mortgages, private lending, or partnerships, can further diversify your risk exposure while maximizing leverage and capital efficiency. Beyond property types and investment strategies, consider factors such as tenant demographics, lease terms, and property management approaches to create a well-rounded and resilient portfolio. For instance, targeting a mix of residential rental properties catering to both young professionals and families can provide stability in occupancy rates and rental income. Additionally, integrating properties with varying maintenance requirements and property management needs can spread your operational responsibilities and mitigate the impact of unforeseen maintenance costs or vacancies. From an overall risk perspective, building a diversified real estate portfolio serves as a protective mechanism against market volatility, economic downturns, and unexpected property-specific challenges. It also enables you to capture opportunities in different segments of the real estate market and optimize your returns in changing economic conditions. Ultimately, the careful curation of a diversified real estate portfolio demands thorough research, diligent analysis, and strategic decision-making but can yield substantial benefits in terms of wealth preservation and long-term financial growth.

Managing Properties: From Tenants to Maintenance

Managing properties involves a multifaceted approach that encompasses various aspects, from tenant relations to property maintenance. Effective property management is essential for maximizing the return on investment and ensuring the long-term success of a real estate portfolio. One of the primary responsibilities of property management is maintaining positive relationships with tenants. This involves providing clear communication, addressing their concerns in a timely manner, and fostering a sense of community within the property. Additionally, establishing fair and consistent rental policies can contribute to tenant satisfaction and retention. Moreover, efficient property maintenance is crucial for preserving the value of the investment. Regular inspections, proactive repairs, and responsive maintenance requests are integral components of property upkeep. It is important to implement a comprehensive maintenance plan to minimize property downtime and uphold its market value. Furthermore, financial management is a key aspect of property management. This includes budgeting for property expenses, collecting rent, and ensuring compliance with financial regulations. Accurate record-keeping and financial transparency are imperative for effective property management, allowing for informed decision-making and strategic planning. Additionally, staying updated on legal regulations and landlord-tenant laws is vital to ensure compliance and mitigate potential risks. Understanding lease agreements, eviction procedures, and fair housing laws is essential for successful property management. Furthermore, leveraging technology for property management can enhance efficiency and productivity. Utilizing property management software for rent collection, maintenance tracking, and tenant communication can streamline operations and improve overall management effectiveness. In conclusion, proficient property management involves balancing tenant relations, property maintenance, financial oversight, legal compliance, and technological innovation. By implementing sound property management practices, real estate investors can safeguard their investments and promote sustainable growth and prosperity within their property portfolios.

Tax Implications and Benefits in Real Estate

Real estate investment offers various tax implications and benefits that can significantly impact an investor's financial position. Understanding these implications is crucial for maximizing returns and minimizing tax liabilities. One of the primary benefits of real estate investment is the ability to leverage tax deductions. Investors can deduct mortgage interest, property taxes, operating expenses, depreciation, and repairs, among other costs, from their taxable income. This not only reduces the amount of income subject to tax but also enhances cash flow from the investment property. Additionally, real estate investors may benefit from favorable capital gains tax treatment. Profits from the sale of investment properties held for more than a year may qualify for long-term capital gains tax rates, which are typically lower than ordinary income tax rates. Furthermore, through a 1031 exchange, investors can defer capital gains taxes by reinvesting the proceeds from the sale of one property into another like-kind property within a specified timeframe. Understanding and utilizing these tax-deferral strategies can help investors grow their real estate portfolios effectively. Moreover, real estate investments offer the potential for significant tax advantages through depreciation. The IRS allows investors to claim depreciation deductions based on the projected useful life of the property improvements. This non-cash deduction can offset rental income, reducing the investor's tax burden while potentially generating positive cash flow. However, it's essential for investors to adhere to tax regulations strictly and maintain accurate records to substantiate these deductions. Failing to do so could result in costly penalties or audits. While real estate investment presents numerous tax benefits, it's vital for investors to stay informed about changes in tax laws and seek professional advice to optimize their tax positions. Working with knowledgeable tax advisors and accountants can help investors navigate complex tax codes, maximize legal deductions, and ensure compliance with reporting requirements. By strategically leveraging tax implications and benefits, real estate investors can enhance their overall investment returns and build long-term wealth.

Mitigating Risks in Real Estate Investment

Mitigating risks is an essential aspect of successful real estate investment. While the potential for substantial returns is a driving force behind real estate investment, it is crucial to recognize and manage the associated risks effectively. This section will delve into various strategies and measures to mitigate risks in real estate investment, offering insights into protecting your investments and maximizing profitability. One fundamental approach to risk mitigation in real estate investment is thorough market research and due diligence. Before committing to any property acquisition, it is vital to conduct comprehensive market analysis, assess the neighborhood's growth potential, evaluate demand drivers, and analyze comparable properties. Additionally, understanding local zoning regulations, environmental factors, and potential legal issues can help identify and mitigate potential risks. Diversification is another key strategy to minimize risks in real estate investment. By spreading investments across different property types or geographic locations, investors can reduce the impact of downturns in specific markets and sectors. Furthermore, diversification can provide insulation against market volatility and economic fluctuations. Effective financial management is integral to risk mitigation in real estate investing. Maintaining adequate liquidity, managing leverage judiciously, and establishing contingency funds for unforeseen expenses contribute to financial resilience and risk reduction. Moreover, prudent budgeting and cost control measures can mitigate financial risks associated with property ownership and management. Engaging professional advisors and leveraging their expertise can be invaluable in mitigating risks in real estate investment. Seeking guidance from experienced real estate agents, attorneys specialized in property law, and financial advisors can offer valuable insights and risk mitigation strategies. Furthermore, building a reliable network of property management professionals, contractors, and maintenance personnel can mitigate operational risks and enhance the efficiency of property management. Finally, staying abreast of regulatory changes, market trends, and emerging technologies is crucial for effective risk management in real estate investment. Adapting to evolving market conditions, embracing innovation, and proactively addressing potential risks can position investors to navigate challenges effectively and capitalize on opportunities for sustainable growth and profitability.

Ways To Make Extra Income

The Art of Writing: From Manuscript to Marketplace

Understanding the Writing Landscape: Genres and Markets

As writers embark on their literary journey, it is essential to comprehend the multifaceted nature of writing genres and the distinct demands of various market segments. The realm of literature is rich and diverse, encompassing genres such as fiction, non-fiction, poetry, drama, science fiction, fantasy, mystery, romance, and many more. Each genre possesses its own unique characteristics, themes, and narrative styles. Understanding these differences is instrumental in tailoring one's work to resonate with the intended audience. Becoming familiar with the nuances of each genre allows writers to harness the appropriate literary techniques, tone, and structure that are integral to captivating readers within that specific niche. Moreover, delving into different genres can expand a writer's creative repertoire, providing opportunities for artistic exploration and personal growth. Furthermore, comprehending the demands of various market segments is crucial for aligning one's writing endeavors with commercial viability. For instance, the expectations of readers in the young adult fiction market may differ significantly from those of readers seeking historical romance novels. Writers must conduct thorough market research to discern the preferences, trends, and purchasing behaviors prevalent within each segment. By doing so, authors can craft content that resonates with their target readership, thus enhancing the likelihood of literary success. Additionally, understanding the demographics and psychographics of potential readers within different genres is essential for honing marketing strategies and establishing a strong author-reader connection. In essence, by immersing themselves in the diverse writing landscape, writers gain valuable insights that empower them to craft compelling narratives that cater to the unique sensibilities of various genres and market segments.

Developing a Unique Voice: The Writer's Signature

Every writer aspires to create work that is not only impactful, but also distinctly their own. Developing a unique voice entails a deep exploration of one's individuality and honing the craft in a way that separates one's writing from the rest. It involves delving into your personal experiences, beliefs, and perspectives, and infusing them into your writing style. Your voice is the literary fingerprint that distinguishes your work from others, making it immediately recognizable to your audience. To begin cultivating your unique voice, it is crucial to understand your strengths and weaknesses as a writer. By recognizing your natural inclinations and tendencies in storytelling, you can harness these attributes to shape your distinct narrative style. Embrace authenticity by incorporating your genuine emotions and distinctive worldview into your writing. This authenticity will resonate with readers and create a deeper connection. An essential aspect of developing a unique voice is to continually refine your language and tone. Experiment with various linguistic devices, explore diverse narrative techniques, and diligently edit your work to ensure that your voice emerges clearly and consistently. Your writing should reflect not only your personal flair, but also your individual perspective on the world around you. Furthermore, immersing yourself in diverse literary works can enrich your own writing style. Study classic literature, contemporary bestsellers, and niche genres to expand your literary horizons. This exposure can inspire fresh ideas and innovative approaches, ultimately contributing to the development of your unique voice. Remember that developing a unique voice is an ongoing process that evolves as you gain experience and insight. Continuously engage with your audience and solicit feedback to gauge their response to your writing style. Embrace constructive criticism and use it as an opportunity to refine and strengthen your voice. Ultimately, by investing time and effort into developing your unique voice, you can establish a lasting impact in the literary world and forge a loyal readership that resonates with your distinct narrative identity.

Crafting Compelling Narratives: Storytelling Techniques

Crafting compelling narratives is at the heart of captivating storytelling, and mastering narrative techniques can elevate a writer's work from good to extraordinary. To achieve this, writers must first understand the fundamental elements that constitute an engaging narrative. This includes a deep comprehension of character development, plot structure, setting, and theme, as well as the art of seamlessly weaving these components together. Character development is a crucial aspect of storytelling, as it involves creating complex, multi-dimensional characters that resonate with readers. By offering insight into their motivations, desires, fears, and flaws, writers can humanize their characters and evoke empathy from their audience. Additionally, understanding the nuances of plot structure is essential in maintaining tension and momentum throughout the narrative. The careful interplay of rising action, climax, and resolution forms the backbone of a well-crafted story, keeping readers engaged and invested throughout. Equally significant is the portrayal of the story's setting, which serves as the backdrop against which the narrative unfolds. Through vivid descriptions and sensory details, writers can transport their readers to immersive and evocative worlds, enhancing the overall reading experience. Furthermore, identifying and exploring central themes allows writers to imbue their narratives with depth and meaning, provoking introspection and contemplation among readers. In addition to understanding these foundational elements, mastering the art of storytelling also involves employing various literary devices and techniques to craft a truly immersive experience for the audience. Techniques such as foreshadowing, symbolism, and dialogue dynamics, when utilized judiciously, add layers of complexity and richness to the narrative, leaving a lasting impression on readers. Moreover, skillful use of pacing and tension-building strategies helps maintain the reader's emotional investment, ensuring that the narrative retains its gripping allure from start to finish. Ultimately, crafting compelling narratives demands a keen understanding of human emotion and experience, allowing writers to infuse authenticity and resonance into their stories. It is through the mastery of storytelling techniques that writers can captivate audiences and leave an indelible imprint on their readers' hearts and minds.

The Manuscript Journey: From Idea to First Draft

Embarking on the manuscript journey is a pivotal stage in the writing process, where ideas begin to take shape as tangible words on the page. It marks the transition from concept to concrete creation, requiring diligence and creativity in equal measure. The inception of a manuscript often stems from a spark of inspiration, an idea or theme that ignites the writer's imagination. As the author delves into this burgeoning concept, they engage in the foundational stage of outlining, where plot structures, characters, and narrative arcs begin to coalesce. This crucial phase demands careful consideration of the story's direction, laying the groundwork for the narrative's evolution.

Moving from the nascent stages of conception, the writer gradually transitions into the act of drafting. Here, the painstaking process of translating ideas into prose takes center stage. It requires a delicate balance between unbridled creativity and methodical execution, as the writer seeks to capture the essence of their vision within the framework of language. The first draft serves as the raw material—rough, unrefined, yet brimming with potential. It's a testament to the perseverance and commitment of the writer, reflecting the dedication required to breathe life into mere thoughts.

Throughout the manuscript journey, discovery becomes a constant companion. As the narrative unfolds, unforeseen plot twists emerge, characters evolve, and themes resonate with newfound clarity. This dynamic evolution imbues the writing process with an exhilarating sense of discovery, where the initial concept transforms into a multifaceted tapestry of storytelling intricacies. The manuscript journey embodies the alchemy of creation, as the author channels creative impulses into a tangible work that resonates with depth and authenticity.

Navigating this transformative odyssey requires unwavering determination and an insatiable appetite for refinement. Each word meticulously chosen, each sentence crafted with intent, each paragraph infused with the author's creative essence. The journey from idea to first draft honours the writer's dedication to their craft, epitomizing the unraveling of narrative threads and the birth of a literary identity. It bridges the chasm between aspiration and actualization, affirming the profound impact of storytelling and the indomitable spirit of the writer.

Editing and Refining: Polishing Your Work for Publication

As you embark on the journey of refining your manuscript for publication, it's crucial to understand the significance of editing in the writing process. Editing is not only about correcting grammatical errors and typos; it involves a comprehensive evaluation of the entire work to enhance its coherence, clarity, and overall impact. The editing process is an opportunity to transform your raw draft into a polished piece that captivates readers and stands out in the competitive literary landscape.

The initial step in the editing phase is self-revision. This involves revisiting your manuscript with a critical eye to identify areas that require improvement. Assess the plot structure, character development, pacing, and consistency of voice and tone. Eliminate redundant scenes, tighten dialogue, and ensure that each chapter contributes meaningfully to the progression of the narrative.

After self-revision, seeking external feedback is invaluable. Beta readers, fellow writers, or professional editors can offer fresh perspectives and constructive criticism. Embrace feedback with an open mind, recognizing that it serves to elevate the quality of your work. Take note of recurring suggestions, but also trust your instincts as the author.

Subsequently, line editing and copyediting come into play. Line editing focuses on the flow of sentences, language use, and stylistic elements. It aims to refine the prose, sharpening descriptions and employing literary devices to heighten the emotional resonance of the writing. Copyediting delves into the technical aspects, addressing grammar, punctuation, and adherence to style guidelines. Both stages demand meticulous attention to detail while preserving the author's unique voice.

Once the content has undergone thorough refinement, consider hiring a professional editor or working with a publishing house's editorial team. An experienced editor brings expertise in identifying nuanced strengths and weaknesses within the manuscript, providing strategic recommendations to elevate the storytelling. Collaborating with an editor fosters a professional relationship centered on mutual respect for the creative vision and a shared commitment to delivering a compelling final product.

Furthermore, engaging in multiple rounds of editing ensures that your work achieves a level of polish that meets industry standards. Publishing a flawless manuscript demonstrates your dedication to excellence, increasing the likelihood of capturing the attention of literary agents, publishers, and discerning readers. Remember, the art of refining your manuscript is an iterative process that demands patience and perseverance, ultimately leading to a manuscript that resonates with authenticity, originality, and literary merit.

Navigating the Publishing World: Traditional vs. Self-Publishing

The decision of how to publish your work is a pivotal one for any aspiring author. Traditionally, publishing involved submitting your manuscript to literary agents or publishing houses and hoping for acceptance. This route often involves a lengthy process, with manuscripts undergoing multiple rounds of editing before even getting to the production and marketing stage. While traditional publishing offers the advantage of professional guidance, wider distribution, and potential advances, it also comes with challenges such as lower royalty rates and less creative control. On the other hand, self-publishing empowers authors to take full control of their work, from editing to design to distribution. With digital platforms like Amazon Kindle Direct Publishing and IngramSpark, self-publishing has become more accessible than ever. Authors retain higher royalties and have the flexibility to set their own publication timeline. However, self-published authors are responsible for their own editing, cover design, marketing, and distribution. Both traditional and self-publishing avenues have their merits and drawbacks, and the right choice depends on your goals, resources, and preferences. Emerging hybrid models offer a middle ground, allowing authors to benefit from professional support while retaining more autonomy. Seeking guidance from experienced authors, industry professionals, and literary communities can provide valuable insights into the best path for your unique writing journey. Understanding the nuances of the publishing landscape is crucial for making informed decisions that align with your creative vision and career aspirations.

Building an Author Platform: Marketing and Branding Yourself

Establishing a strong author platform is essential for aspiring writers looking to carve a successful path in the literary world. This encompasses the strategic development of an author's brand, online presence, and overall visibility within their target audience. To accomplish this, one must first define their unique value proposition—what sets them apart in a sea of writers. Crafting a compelling author bio that encapsulates their background, passions, and writing journey serves as a solid foundation for their brand. Additionally, authors must harness the power of social media platforms to engage with potential readers, share insights about their writing process, and provide a glimpse into their personal lives. Creating a professional website or blog can further enhance an author's digital presence, serving as a hub for their literary work, upcoming releases, and engaging content. Building an email list is also crucial, allowing direct communication with a loyal reader base and facilitating outreach for book launches and promotions. Collaborating with book influencers, bloggers, and fellow authors can broaden an author's reach and foster valuable connections within the literary community. Leveraging speaking engagements, workshops, and book readings presents opportunities to connect with audiences on a more personal level, solidifying the author's place in their niche. Harnessing the potential of book signings and literary events can further amplify an author's visibility, providing avenues for direct interaction with readers and book enthusiasts. Embracing a consistent and authentic brand voice across all platforms cultivates recognition and fosters trust among readers. This comprehensive approach to building an author platform not only enhances an author's visibility but also lays a formidable groundwork for driving book sales, cultivating a dedicated readership, and establishing a lasting legacy within the literary landscape.

Monetizing Your Work: Rights, Royalties, and Revenue Streams

Monetizing your writing requires a comprehensive understanding of the rights, royalties, and various revenue streams that can be leveraged in the ever-evolving publishing landscape. As an author, securing the rights to your work is paramount in ensuring that you can capitalize on its commercial potential. These rights typically include the right to reproduce your work, distribute it, and create derivative works based on your original content. Understanding these legal aspects and working with a literary agent or legal counsel can safeguard your interests and maximize your earnings. Royalties, another crucial aspect of monetization, come in different forms such as advance payments, flat fees, or a percentage of book sales. It's essential to comprehend the intricacies of royalty structures and negotiate favorable terms with publishers or distributors to optimize your financial returns. Furthermore, diversifying revenue streams beyond traditional book sales can significantly enhance your income. Opportunities exist in audiobooks, film or television adaptations, merchandise licensing, speaking engagements, and even affiliate marketing through recommendations of relevant products or services within your writing. Exploring these alternative revenue avenues demands strategic planning and negotiation skills to secure profitable deals. Additionally, harnessing digital platforms and social media can offer new avenues for monetization by creating exclusive content for subscription-based models or leveraging crowdfunding platforms to fund passion projects. Embracing emerging technologies and adapting to new consumption trends enables authors to tap into unconventional revenue sources. Ultimately, successful monetization relies not only on producing compelling content but also on shrewd business acumen and proactive engagement with industry professionals. By mastering the art of rights management, optimizing royalty agreements, and innovating across diverse revenue streams, writers can effectively translate their literary prowess into sustainable financial rewards.

Engaging Readers: Community Building and Audience Engagement

Engaging readers goes beyond just writing compelling stories; it involves building a community of dedicated fans and establishing meaningful connections with your audience. Successful writers understand the value of cultivating relationships with their readers, as this can lead to increased book sales, positive word-of-mouth referrals, and ongoing support for their work.

Community building begins by actively participating in literary events, book clubs, and writing workshops. Engaging with readers in person or virtually allows you to understand their preferences, gain insights into current trends, and receive direct feedback on your writing. By creating a dialogue with your audience, you can foster a sense of belonging and loyalty, thereby strengthening the bond between author and reader.

In addition to personal interactions, leveraging digital platforms is crucial for audience engagement. Social media channels, author websites, and blogging platforms offer avenues to share exclusive content, behind-the-scenes glimpses, and updates on upcoming projects. Establishing a consistent online presence enables readers to connect with you beyond the pages of your book, creating a dynamic and interactive experience that enhances their investment in your writing.

Moreover, encouraging reader participation through contests, Q&A sessions, and virtual book launches fosters a sense of inclusivity and excitement among your audience. By involving readers in the creative process, you not only deepen their engagement but also inspire them to become advocates for your work. This grassroots support can have a tangible impact on book sales and overall brand visibility.

Collaborating with local bookstores, libraries, and literary communities further reinforces reader engagement. Hosting book signings, author talks, and writing workshops provides opportunities for face-to-face interactions and establishes a strong rapport with your fan base. These engagements help position you as a relatable and accessible figure, elevating your connection with readers and creating lasting impressions.

Ultimately, engaging readers is an ongoing commitment that extends beyond book releases. By prioritizing community building and audience engagement, you can forge meaningful connections, nurture a loyal following, and lay the foundation for a sustainable and thriving writing career.

Adapting to Industry Trends: Staying Relevant as a Writer

As the writing landscape continues to evolve, it is imperative for writers to adapt to industry trends in order to remain relevant and competitive. The digital age has revolutionized the way content is consumed, leading to shifts in reader preferences and publishing platforms. With this in mind, writers must proactively adjust their approach to cater to the changing needs of the audience. First and foremost, staying abreast of technological advancements and digital tools is essential. From social media platforms to self-publishing services, embracing new technologies can enhance a writer's visibility and reach. Additionally, understanding and utilizing data analytics can provide invaluable insights into reader demographics, reading habits, and market trends. By leveraging this information, writers can tailor their content to resonate with their target audience, thereby increasing their relevance in the literary sphere. Moreover, keeping an eye on emerging genres and themes is crucial. The public's interests are dynamic, and writers must be attuned to current cultural, social, and political movements to produce works that resonate with contemporary readers. This may involve exploring diverse storytelling formats, addressing pressing societal issues, or incorporating innovative narrative techniques. Furthermore, collaboration and networking within the writing community are paramount. Engaging with fellow writers, editors, publishers, and literary agents not only fosters professional growth but also provides exposure to fresh perspectives and industry insights. By building meaningful connections, writers can stay informed about upcoming opportunities, market demands, and collaborative projects, enhancing their adaptability and relevance. Additionally, cultivating a strong online presence through blogging, podcasting, or vlogging enables writers to engage with audiences directly and participate in relevant discussions. This active engagement can foster a loyal readership and establish the writer as an authority in their niche. Lastly, embracing continuous learning and evolving skill sets is fundamental. Whether through attending writing workshops, pursuing further education in related fields, or seeking out mentors, writers can refine their craft and remain adaptable in an ever-changing landscape. Adapting to industry trends is not merely about conforming to popular fads, but rather about honing one's creativity and expertise to meet the evolving demands of the literary market. By embracing innovation, embracing collaboration, and pursuing ongoing self-improvement, writers can position themselves as valuable contributors in the dynamic world of literature.

Ways To Make Extra Income

Crafting and Selling: Turning Art into Income

Understanding the Market for Crafts

The crafts market is a dynamic and diverse industry that offers numerous opportunities for skilled artisans and creators. To thrive in this competitive landscape, it is crucial to gain a deep understanding of the market trends and demands. By staying informed about current consumer preferences, emerging styles, and popular themes, crafters can identify potential opportunities and tailor their products to meet market demands. Exploring the latest trends in the crafts market provides valuable insights into what resonates with consumers and enables artisans to create unique, in-demand offerings. As the market evolves, certain niches may experience increased demand, such as eco-friendly or sustainable crafts, personalized merchandise, or artisanal goods. By keeping a pulse on these trends, crafters can position themselves strategically to capitalize on emerging opportunities. Moreover, understanding the market for crafts involves researching consumer behaviors, including purchasing patterns, preferred sales channels, and target demographics. This knowledge allows crafters to fine-tune their marketing strategies, product offerings, and pricing to align with consumer preferences. Additionally, by analyzing market dynamics, artisans can identify potential gaps or unmet needs within specific craft categories, paving the way for innovative product development and differentiation. In conclusion, a comprehensive understanding of the crafts market empowers artisans to adapt to evolving consumer preferences, leverage emerging trends, and position their craft businesses for sustained success.

Identifying Your Niche in Art and Craft

In the world of art and craft, finding your niche is crucial to not only stand out in a crowded marketplace but also to cater to a specific audience that resonates with your creations. Identifying your niche involves understanding your unique artistic style, your personal interests, and the market demand for specific types of crafts. A niche can be defined by various factors such as the materials used, the theme or subject matter, the intended use of the craft, or even the target demographic.

To begin identifying your niche, start by reflecting on your own creativity and passion. What types of crafts do you excel at creating? What themes or styles do you naturally gravitate towards? Understanding your strengths and inclinations will help you narrow down potential niches that align with your artistic vision. Additionally, consider conducting market research to identify gaps or trends in the art and craft industry. This may involve studying popular platforms like Etsy or attending local craft fairs to observe consumer preferences and purchasing behaviors.

Another important aspect of identifying your niche is to assess the competition within your chosen craft category. Who are your competitors? What sets your work apart from theirs? By evaluating the strengths and weaknesses of existing players in your niche, you can position yourself strategically and carve out a distinct space for your creations. Moreover, analyzing customer feedback and reviews on similar products can provide valuable insights into what resonates with buyers and what areas may offer opportunities for innovation and differentiation.

Furthermore, it's essential to consider the practical aspects of your chosen niche, such as the availability of resources, the production scalability, and the profit potential. While passion is a driving force in any creative endeavor, a successful niche should also align with the economic viability of your craft. Assess the cost and feasibility of producing crafts within your chosen niche, as well as the pricing dynamics and overall market demand.

Ultimately, identifying your niche in art and craft is an introspective and analytical process that combines self-awareness, market knowledge, and a keen understanding of your artistic capabilities. By pinpointing a niche that resonates with both your creativity and market demand, you pave the way for establishing a distinctive presence in the art and craft landscape, fostering meaningful connections with your audience, and translating your passion into a sustainable income stream.

Developing Unique and Marketable Products

In the journey of turning art into income, the development of unique and marketable products is a crucial step that demands creativity, expertise, and strategic thinking. To stand out in a crowded market, artisans must strive to create products that not only showcase their craftsmanship but also resonate with their target audience. This process begins with thorough market research and trend analysis to identify gaps or opportunities in the current landscape of art and craft. Understanding consumer preferences and emerging trends allows artisans to tailor their creations to meet the demands of potential buyers, ultimately increasing the marketability of their products. Moreover, developing a unique selling proposition (USP) sets one's offerings apart from competitors and acts as a compelling reason for customers to choose their products over others. Whether it's innovative design, superior quality, or a distinct artistic style, identifying and accentuating a USP forms the foundation for creating a strong product identity. Additionally, the fusion of traditional craftsmanship with modern aesthetics or functionalities can infuse products with a sense of timelessness and practicality, adding value and appeal. It's imperative to continuously innovate and experiment with new techniques, materials, and styles to keep the product line fresh and engaging. Embracing sustainability and ethical sourcing practices further enhances the desirability of artisanal products, aligning with the growing consumer preference for responsible consumption. From eco-friendly materials to socially conscious production methods, integrating ethical considerations into the product development phase can elevate the perceived value of the offerings. Collaborations with other artists, designers, or complementary brands can also result in the creation of unique, limited-edition products that cater to niche markets and collector segments. By fostering creativity and leveraging inspiration from diverse sources, artisans can breathe life into their creations, making them not just items to be bought, but stories to be cherished and shared. Ultimately, the meticulous process of developing unique and marketable products is an art form in itself, intertwining passion, skill, and commercial acumen to craft offerings that captivate the heart and ignite the imagination of consumers.

Sourcing Quality Materials and Tools

Every artisan knows the fundamental importance of sourcing high-quality materials and tools for their craft. The process of selecting the right materials and tools is a critical factor that directly impacts the quality, appeal, and value of the final product. When it comes to crafting and selling art, attention to detail in material selection can make all the difference in gaining an edge in the market.

The first step in sourcing high-quality materials and tools is to prioritize durability, authenticity, and uniqueness. Whether creating handmade jewelry, woodworking, ceramics, or any other craft, it is essential to invest time and effort in finding materials that exude quality and stand out in the finished piece. Consider partnering with reputable suppliers and vendors who share your commitment to excellence. By doing so, you can ensure a consistent supply of superior materials that align with your artistic vision and brand values.

Furthermore, sustainability and ethical sourcing are increasingly valued in today's market. Consumers are becoming more conscious of the environmental and ethical impact of their purchases. As such, sourcing materials from sustainable and ethical sources not only adds value to your products but also contributes to a positive brand image. Embracing eco-friendly materials and supporting fair trade practices can resonate with conscientious consumers, setting your creations apart in the competitive marketplace.

It is also crucial to have a keen eye for detail when selecting tools for your craft. Investing in top-notch tools that are tailored to your specific needs can streamline the production process and elevate the quality of your work. Whether it's precision cutting tools for intricate designs, specialized brushes for fine art, or state-of-the-art equipment for larger-scale projects, the right tools can enhance efficiency and craftsmanship. Keep abreast of the latest technological advancements and innovations in craft tools, as staying at the forefront of tool technology can give you an advantage in both production and product quality.

Lastly, establishing strong relationships with suppliers and staying informed about market trends and innovations in materials and tools is imperative for sustaining a successful arts and crafts business. Cultivating these relationships can lead to exclusive access to new materials and tools, fostering a competitive advantage. Additionally, continuous research and exploration of emerging materials and tools enable you to adapt and innovate, ensuring that your offerings remain fresh, distinctive, and appealing to your target audience.

Mastering the Craft of Production

In the journey of turning art into income, mastering the craft of production is an essential step to ensure the consistent quality and efficiency of your creative process. From creating handmade goods to producing art prints or digital products, the production phase demands attention to detail and a commitment to excellence. This section will delve into the intricacies of honing your production skills and maximizing output while maintaining the integrity of your artistic vision.

To begin with, streamlining your production processes involves meticulous planning and organization. Assess the workflow of creating your crafts or art and identify areas where improvements can be made. Whether it's optimizing the assembly line for handmade products or refining the digital design process, implementing efficient production methods can significantly enhance productivity.

Moreover, embracing technology and automation can revolutionize your production capabilities. Utilizing advanced tools and software, such as design programs and production machinery, can expedite the manufacturing process without compromising on quality. Additionally, integrating automation where feasible can free up time for creative ideation and business development, ultimately fostering sustainable growth.

Furthermore, quality control is paramount in mastering the craft of production. Implementing stringent quality checks at every stage of production helps uphold the standards that define your brand. Inspecting materials, scrutinizing workmanship, and testing finished products are vital steps to ensure that only the finest creations reach your customers, thereby building trust and credibility within your market.

Effective inventory management also plays a crucial role in production mastery. Balancing supply and demand, minimizing excess stock, and optimizing storage solutions are imperative to avoid bottlenecks in the production cycle while controlling costs. By employing sound inventory management practices, you can achieve a harmonious equilibrium between meeting customer orders and avoiding overstock situations.

Finally, fostering a culture of continuous improvement within your production processes is key to staying ahead in the competitive landscape. Encouraging feedback from both customers and internal teams, investing in ongoing training for production staff, and staying abreast of industry advancements are all integral parts of refining and enhancing your craft of production. Embracing innovation and adaptability ensures that your production methods remain agile and responsive to changing market dynamics, thereby bolstering long-term success.

Online Platforms: Reaching a Global Audience

Craftsmanship is an art, but it's also a business. In today's interconnected world, aspiring artisans have at their disposal an array of powerful online platforms to showcase and sell their creations to a global audience. Online platforms such as Etsy, Amazon Handmade, and eBay provide artists and crafters with the opportunity to present their work to millions of potential customers. These platforms offer user-friendly interfaces and tools to set up an online store, list products, and manage sales. With the rise of social media and e-commerce, marketing your crafts has never been easier or more accessible. Utilizing digital marketing techniques such as search engine optimization (SEO), social media advertising, and influencer partnerships, creators can amplify their reach and attract customers from all corners of the globe. Establishing a strong online presence through engaging content, captivating photography, and compelling product descriptions is essential to stand out in a crowded marketplace. Embracing the power of storytelling can create emotional connections with potential buyers, giving them an insight into the creativity and dedication behind each piece. Crafting a unique brand image and establishing a coherent brand story can significantly impact consumer perception and loyalty. Providing exceptional customer service and fostering a sense of community around your brand can turn one-time buyers into loyal advocates. Understanding the dynamics of international shipping, customs, and import taxes is crucial when targeting a global audience. Offering transparent and reliable shipping options, along with clear communication regarding potential additional costs, builds trust and ensures a smooth purchasing experience for customers worldwide. Embracing technology and leveraging data analytics can provide valuable insights into customer behavior, preferences, and market trends. These insights can inform product development, pricing strategies, and marketing decisions. As an artisan, grasping the power of online platforms and e-commerce not only expands your reach but also empowers you to compete on a global scale, turning your passion into a sustainable source of income.

Pricing Strategies: Balancing Art and Profit

In the world of crafting and selling, pricing your products is a critical aspect that can greatly impact the success of your business. Finding the delicate balance between valuing your artistry and ensuring profitability is essential for sustained growth and customer satisfaction. When setting prices for your crafts, it's imperative to consider various factors such as material costs, labor, overhead expenses, market demand, and your brand positioning.

First and foremost, understanding the total cost of production is pivotal. This includes not only the direct costs of materials and tools but also incidental costs like utilities, packaging, and marketing. By calculating these expenses accurately, you can ascertain a baseline price that covers all costs while leaving room for profit.

Additionally, it's important to analyze the market and assess the perceived value of your crafts. Research comparable products in the market and evaluate their pricing strategies. Consider the uniqueness and quality of your crafts in comparison to others and adjust your pricing accordingly to reflect the value you offer.

Furthermore, implementing a tiered pricing structure can be advantageous. By offering a range of products at different price points, you cater to a broader spectrum of customers with varying budgets. This not only widens your customer base but also allows you to capture different segments of the market.

Another effective strategy is to incorporate storytelling into your pricing. By sharing the story behind each crafted piece, you enhance its perceived value, making customers more willing to pay a premium price. Highlighting the craftsmanship, inspiration, and dedication invested in creating the product adds a layer of emotional connection, resulting in increased desirability.

Moreover, periodic review and adjustment of pricing is essential. As your business evolves and your brand gains recognition, your pricing strategies should evolve as well. Regularly evaluating the market, consumer behavior, and competition enables you to adapt and optimize your pricing to maximize revenue and maintain competitiveness.

Lastly, transparency in pricing is paramount in building trust with your customers. Clearly communicate the reasons behind your pricing, demonstrating the fair value of your crafts, and fostering a sense of integrity. Customers appreciate honesty and clarity, and transparent pricing can lead to enhanced credibility and customer loyalty.

By incorporating these pricing strategies thoughtfully, you can strike a harmonious balance between honoring the artistic value of your crafts and ensuring sustainable profitability within your business.

Marketing Your Crafts Effectively

Marketing your crafts effectively is crucial in today's competitive landscape. It involves a strategic blend of online and offline efforts to create visibility, build brand recognition, and ultimately drive sales. One of the first steps in an effective marketing strategy is to establish a strong online presence. This includes having a professional website showcasing your crafts, regular posts on social media platforms, and engaging with potential customers through email newsletters or blog content. Leveraging e-commerce platforms and marketplaces can also expand your reach to a wider audience. Using high-quality visuals and storytelling in your marketing materials will help to create an emotional connection with your audience, which can be a powerful tool in driving sales. Traditional offline channels should not be overlooked, as participation in craft fairs, local markets, and pop-up shops can offer valuable face-to-face interaction with potential customers. Establishing partnerships with local businesses or galleries can also provide additional exposure for your crafts. A successful marketing strategy involves understanding your target audience and tailoring your messaging to their preferences and interests. Conducting market research and analyzing customer behavior can provide valuable insights that can inform your marketing approach. It's important to engage with your customers beyond the initial purchase. Building long-term relationships and fostering loyalty can be achieved through exceptional customer service, personalized communications, and offering exclusive perks or promotions. Encouraging customer reviews and testimonials can also bolster your credibility and attract new customers. Networking within the crafting community and collaborating with complementary businesses can open up new marketing opportunities and further expand your reach. In summary, effective marketing for your crafts requires a multi-faceted approach, encompassing digital, traditional, and relationship-focused strategies, all centered around understanding and connecting with your target audience.

Building Customer Relationships and Loyalty

Building strong customer relationships is the cornerstone of any successful business, and the world of crafts is no different. When you offer a product that is infused with your passion and creativity, it becomes essential to connect with your customers on a personal level, creating trust and loyalty in the process. In today's competitive marketplace, fostering meaningful relationships with your clientele can set you apart and drive long-term success. To achieve this, it is crucial to prioritize customer satisfaction at every touchpoint of their journey with your brand. As a craftsperson, taking the time to understand your customers' needs and preferences can go a long way in tailoring your products and services to exceed their expectations. Transparency and open communication are also key elements in cultivating a strong bond with your audience. By being honest about your processes, materials, and pricing, you can build credibility and earn the trust of your customers.

Additionally, going the extra mile in providing exceptional customer service can leave a lasting impression and encourage repeat business. This could involve offering personalized recommendations, responding promptly to inquiries, or even providing after-sales support. Moreover, utilizing social media and other digital platforms to maintain an ongoing dialogue with your customer base can humanize your brand and foster a sense of community. Engaging with customers through these channels not only allows for direct feedback but also provides opportunities to showcase the craftsmanship behind your creations and share the stories that inspire your work. Another effective strategy for nurturing customer loyalty is to express appreciation for their support and patronage. Small gestures such as handwritten thank-you notes, exclusive offers, or inviting them to behind-the-scenes events can make customers feel valued and part of a special community. Loyalty programs and rewards for repeat purchases can also incentivize customers to continue choosing your brand over others. Lastly, always seek feedback and learn from your customers' experiences. Constructive criticism can be invaluable in improving your offerings and refining your approach to better serve their needs. By continuously working on building and maintaining strong customer relationships, you can establish a loyal following that not only sustains your business but also advocates for your brand, driving organic growth through positive word-of-mouth. Ultimately, investing in these relationships will not only foster a dedicated customer base but also create opportunities for collaborations, referrals, and sustained success in the ever-evolving craft market.

Scaling Up: From Hobby to Full-Time Business

Transitioning from a hobbyist to a full-time business owner in the craft industry requires strategic planning and deliberate actions. As you aim to scale up your craft business, it is crucial to focus on several key areas that will enable sustainable growth and success. Firstly, consider the operational aspects of your business. Evaluate your production capacity, streamline your processes, and invest in tools and equipment that can increase efficiency without compromising quality. Additionally, assess your existing supply chain and explore opportunities for partnerships or bulk purchasing to optimize costs. Moreover, developing a robust online presence and e-commerce infrastructure is imperative for transitioning into a full-time business. This involves creating a professional website, implementing secure payment systems, and establishing a seamless order fulfillment process. Leveraging social media and digital marketing strategies will also be pivotal in expanding your reach and attracting a broader customer base. Furthermore, as you scale up, prioritizing financial management becomes increasingly critical. Implementing accounting software, setting clear budgetary guidelines, and regularly reviewing your pricing strategy and profit margins will help maintain financial stability and support future growth. Building a team can significantly enhance your capacity and capabilities as a growing business. Whether it involves hiring employees, collaborating with freelancers, or outsourcing certain tasks, assembling a competent and dedicated team can alleviate workload pressures and drive productivity. Finally, don't overlook the importance of continuous innovation and adaptation. Stay abreast of industry trends, explore new creative techniques, and solicit feedback from customers to refine your offerings. Embracing change and evolution will fuel your business's competitiveness and relevance in the market. By methodically addressing these considerations and embracing the challenges of entrepreneurship, you can effectively elevate your craft from a passion project to a thriving full-time enterprise.

Ways To Make Extra Income

Flipping Goods: Repair, Resell, Repeat

Understanding the Basics of Flipping: An Introduction

Understanding the basics of flipping involves delving into fundamental concepts and terminologies used in the world of product flipping. To excel in this field, individuals need to comprehend the dynamics of supply and demand, pricing strategies, market trends, and consumer behavior. In essence, flipping pertains to the art of purchasing undervalued items and subsequently reselling them at a higher price, thereby generating profit margins. The ability to identify potential bargain opportunities, assess their market value, and successfully execute the resale process is essential for a fruitful flipping endeavor.

Market research serves as a cornerstone in this process, enabling flippers to stay informed about current trends, emerging demand, and customer preferences. By scrutinizing market data and consumer behavior, flippers can gain insights that aid in determining which products hold potential for successful flipping. This necessitates keeping a close eye on market trends, economic indicators, and industry developments to capitalize on lucrative opportunities.

Furthermore, understanding the terminology used in the marketplace is pivotal for effective communication and decision-making. Concepts such as wholesale pricing, retail arbitrage, bundle sales, and niche markets are integral to comprehending the nuances of the flipping landscape. Familiarity with these terms empowers individuals to engage in strategic negotiations, establish profitable partnerships, and diversify their product portfolio.

Moreover, identifying scalable niches and diversifying across various categories can mitigate risks and maximize the potential for successful flips. For instance, while some may find success in vintage clothing, others may excel in electronic gadgets or collectible items. Utilizing analytical tools and resources to gauge the demand for specific categories or products can significantly contribute to a comprehensive understanding of market segments and consumer behavior.

In conclusion, mastering the fundamentals of flipping demands insight into the complexities of market dynamics, consumer behavior, and strategic decision-making. By aligning with market trends, understanding terminologies, and exploring untapped niches, individuals can lay the groundwork for a thriving flipping business venture.

Identifying Profitable Goods: Market Research and Trends

In the realm of flipping goods, success hinges on the ability to identify potentially profitable items through astute market research and a deep understanding of evolving consumer trends. To embark on this journey, it's crucial to immerse oneself in the dynamics of various markets, ranging from vintage collectibles to contemporary gadgets. Through diligent research, one can discern the items that possess the potential for substantial resale value, thereby setting the stage for lucrative endeavors. Engaging in meticulous market research involves analyzing sales data, customer preferences, and emerging trends. This critical evaluation allows aspiring entrepreneurs to stay ahead of the curve and make informed decisions when sourcing products for resale. It also involves keeping a close eye on industry publications, attending relevant trade shows, and leveraging digital platforms to gauge the pulse of the market. By actively monitoring fluctuating demand and price dynamics, flippers can position themselves as shrewd arbiters of market trends. Moreover, understanding the nuances of seasonal demand and recognizing upcoming fads are integral aspects of this endeavor. For instance, identifying the resurgence of retro fashion trends or the growing interest in sustainable products can provide valuable insights into the types of goods that hold significant potential in the resale market. By harmonizing astute market research with a forward-thinking approach, flippers can unearth hidden gems that resonate with both their target audience and overarching consumer preferences. Ultimately, the art of identifying profitable goods lies at the intersection of perceptive data analysis and the innate capacity to anticipate consumer inclinations in an ever-evolving marketplace.

Sourcing Products: Where to Find Hidden Gems

Often, the success of a flipping venture hinges on the ability to source high-quality products at favorable prices. To find hidden gems for your flipping business, it's crucial to explore a multifaceted approach to sourcing. One effective method is scouring estate sales and auctions, where overlooked treasures can be acquired at competitive rates. Online platforms, such as eBay, Craigslist, and Facebook Marketplace, also serve as valuable sources for locating unique items with potential for value appreciation. Additionally, building relationships with local thrift stores, flea markets, and garage sales can provide access to a diverse range of products ripe for flipping. Collaborating with wholesalers and liquidation companies presents yet another avenue for acquiring inventory at discounted rates. Furthermore, cultivating a network of contacts within the industry can unearth exclusive opportunities for sourcing rare and desirable items. Keep in mind, creativity and out-of-the-box thinking often lead to remarkable discoveries—consider reaching out to manufacturers, artisans, or even abandoned storage units for potential one-of-a-kind finds. When sourcing products, always stay attuned to market demands and consumer preferences to ensure that the items you acquire align with current trends and have the potential for profitable resale. By diversifying your sourcing channels and embracing innovative strategies, you can consistently uncover unique, high-value goods while staying ahead in the competitive world of flipping.

Repair and Restoration Techniques: Adding Value to Your Finds

In the world of flipping goods, the ability to breathe new life into worn or damaged items is a fundamental skill that sets successful flippers apart. When it comes to adding value to your finds, mastering repair and restoration techniques is an art form in itself. Whether it's furniture, electronics, vintage clothing, or other secondhand treasures, understanding how to revitalize these items can significantly increase their appeal and market value. One of the key aspects of this process is to thoroughly assess the condition of each item and identify areas that require attention. From patching up scratches and dents to repairing electrical components, every meticulous effort contributes to enhancing the overall quality of the product. Additionally, having a comprehensive toolkit equipped with the necessary supplies for sanding, painting, reupholstering, and refurbishing is vital for executing these tasks effectively. Furthermore, familiarizing oneself with various materials and methodologies for restoration allows for versatility when encountering diverse types of products. For example, knowing how to treat different wood finishes, mend fabric tears, or fix electronic malfunctions expands the range of items one can confidently tackle. Moreover, it's crucial to strike a balance between preserving the item's original charm and infusing personalized improvements. By layering creativity with practicality, you can transform a weathered piece into a sought-after gem while retaining its authentic character. Embracing eco-friendly practices such as upcycling and repurposing also aligns with contemporary consumer preferences and adds an ethical dimension to the process. Lastly, documenting the journey of transformation through compelling before-and-after visuals not only showcases your expertise but also resonates with potential buyers on an emotive level. By honing your skills in repair and restoration, you have the power to give forgotten objects a new narrative and unlock their profit potential in the marketplace.

Valuation Perspectives: Pricing Strategies That Work

As a savvy entrepreneur in the flipping industry, one of the most critical aspects of your business is the ability to accurately price your products. Valuation perspectives play a pivotal role in determining the success of your flipping endeavors. To effectively set the right prices, it's imperative to consider various factors that contribute to the perceived value of your goods. When assessing the pricing of your items, take into account the current market demand and trends. Conduct thorough research to understand the pricing benchmarks for similar products in the market. This comparative analysis will provide valuable insights on setting competitive yet profitable prices for your flips. Additionally, evaluating the condition and quality of your goods is paramount in determining their worth.

Items that have undergone meticulous repair and restoration should command a premium, reflecting the added value resulting from your skilled craftsmanship. Conversely, items in pristine condition should also be priced accordingly to attract discerning buyers willing to pay for well-maintained merchandise. Consider the uniqueness and rarity of your finds when pricing them. Rare or one-of-a-kind items often justify higher price points, appealing to collectors and enthusiasts who appreciate exclusivity. Moreover, take into consideration the cost of acquisition, restoration, and any associated overheads when setting prices. It's essential to factor in these expenses to ensure that your pricing not only covers costs but also yields a desirable profit margin. The psychology of pricing cannot be overstated. Understanding consumer behavior and purchasing triggers can inform effective pricing strategies. Utilize pricing techniques such as charm pricing (e.g., $19.99 instead of $20) or bundling related items to create perceived value and incentivize purchases. Furthermore, strategic pricing promotions, limited-time offers, and tiered pricing structures can stimulate customer engagement and drive sales. Leveraging online platforms and marketplaces grants access to valuable data and analytics. Utilize these insights to optimize pricing strategies based on customer demographics, geographic regions, and historical buying patterns. Adaptive pricing, where prices dynamically adjust based on demand and other external factors, can enhance competitiveness and maximize revenue. In conclusion, mastering valuation perspectives and implementing dynamic pricing strategies are integral to the success of your flipping business. By diligently considering market trends, product quality, uniqueness, costs, consumer behavior, and leveraging data-driven insights, you can confidently price your items to capture value and foster sustained profitability.

Effective Marketing and Sales Tactics: Attracting the Right Buyers

To successfully attract the right buyers when engaging in goods flipping, it is crucial to employ effective marketing and sales tactics. The ability to target the most suitable audience for your products can significantly impact the success of your venture. Utilizing a multi-faceted approach, encompassing both online and offline strategies, can help maximize exposure and drive sales.

An essential aspect of attracting the right buyers is creating compelling product listings that highlight the unique features and value propositions of the items you are selling. Rich, detailed descriptions accompanied by high-quality images can captivate potential buyers and pique their interest. Ensuring that your listings are optimized with relevant keywords can also enhance visibility on online platforms and search engines.

Incorporating social media into your marketing efforts can yield impressive results. Leveraging platforms such as Instagram, Facebook, and Pinterest enables you to showcase your curated products to a wide audience, engage with potential customers, and harness the power of visual storytelling to convey the desirability of your offerings. Engaging with followers through interactive posts, behind-the-scenes content, and user-generated testimonials can foster a sense of community and trust around your brand.

Furthermore, establishing partnerships with influencers or relevant bloggers can amplify your reach and credibility. Collaborating with individuals who align with your brand ethos and have a dedicated following can introduce your products to new demographics and bolster brand recognition.

In addition to digital marketing, traditional sales tactics should not be overlooked. Participating in local markets, pop-up events, or craft fairs can provide valuable face-to-face interactions with potential buyers and allow them to experience the quality and uniqueness of your products firsthand. Building relationships with your customer base and actively seeking feedback can cultivate loyalty and drive repeat purchases.

It is imperative to constantly monitor and analyze the performance of your marketing and sales initiatives. Utilizing data analytics and insights from platform metrics can offer valuable information about customer behavior, preferences, and conversion rates. This data-driven approach enables you to refine your strategies, optimize your campaigns, and capitalize on emerging trends.

By combining these diverse marketing and sales tactics, you can effectively attract the right buyers and foster sustained interest in your flipped goods, ultimately driving profitability and long-term success.

Navigating Online Platforms: Maximizing Reach and Efficiency

In today's digital age, the power of online platforms in maximizing reach and efficiency cannot be overstated. Whether you're a seasoned entrepreneur or just starting out in the world of flipping goods, understanding how to navigate these platforms effectively is crucial for success. With a myriad of options available, from established marketplaces like eBay and Amazon to niche platforms such as Chairish and Poshmark, the key lies in strategically selecting the right platforms that align with your target audience and product niche. Each platform comes with its unique set of features, tools, and audience demographics. Thus, it's essential to conduct thorough research to ensure that your chosen platforms resonate with your brand and offerings. Maximizing reach involves embracing various strategies, including optimizing product listings with high-quality images and compelling descriptions, leveraging keywords for improved searchability, and actively engaging with potential buyers through comments, direct messages, and promotional offers. Utilizing paid advertising and sponsored placements can further extend your reach and visibility to a wider audience, amplifying your opportunities for successful sales. Efficiency is equally paramount when navigating online platforms. Streamlining inventory management, order processing, and customer communication are vital components to ensure a seamless and professional experience for buyers. Leveraging automation tools and integrating with shipping solutions can simplify logistical tasks, allowing you to focus more on sourcing, marketing, and growing your flipping venture. Additionally, harnessing data analytics provided by these platforms can offer valuable insights into consumer behavior, popular trends, and performance metrics, enabling informed decision-making to optimize your operations. Keeping abreast of platform updates, policy changes, and best practices is crucial to stay competitive and adapt to evolving market dynamics. Networking with other sellers, joining relevant forums, and attending virtual events can provide invaluable knowledge sharing and support within the online flipping community. Ultimately, navigating online platforms effectively is about striking a balance between maximizing your reach and ensuring operational efficiency, all while maintaining a strong brand identity and delivering exceptional value to your customers.

Building a Brand: Establishing Credibility and Trust

When it comes to the art of flipping goods, establishing a strong brand presence is essential for sustained success. Building a brand goes beyond simply having a unique logo or catchy tagline; it involves creating an identity that resonates with your target market and sets you apart from competitors. This section will delve into the strategies and tactics necessary to imbue your flipping venture with credibility and trust. The first step in building a brand is to define your mission and values. What do you stand for as a flipper? Are you committed to providing high-quality, sustainable products? Do you prioritize excellent customer service and transparency in your business dealings? By clearly articulating your core values, you can begin to establish an authentic brand that garners trust and loyalty. Visual identity plays a crucial role in brand building. Your logo, color scheme, and overall aesthetic should be consistent across all touchpoints, from your online platforms to your packaging. Consistency breeds recognition, and recognition leads to trust. Additionally, crafting compelling brand storytelling can deepen connections with your audience. Share the journey of how your flipping business came to be, highlight the stories behind your best finds, and showcase the positive impact your brand has made within the community. Aligning your brand with social and environmental causes can also enhance credibility, as consumers increasingly seek out businesses that demonstrate a commitment to ethical practices. Leveraging influencer partnerships and customer testimonials further reinforces the trustworthiness of your brand. When influencers or satisfied customers endorse your products, it amplifies the confidence that potential buyers have in your offerings. Lastly, delivering a superior customer experience is paramount in solidifying your brand's reputation. Responsive communication, seamless transactions, and prompt order fulfillment all contribute to positive perceptions of your brand. By prioritizing consistent quality and reliability, you fortify the trust that customers place in your flipping enterprise. Ultimately, through intentional brand development, your flipping venture can evolve into a respected and reputable force in the market, fostering long-term relationships with loyal customers and partners.

Case Studies of Successful Flipping: Lessons and Inspirations

In this section, we will delve into real-life case studies of successful flipping endeavors, providing invaluable insights and inspirations for aspiring entrepreneurs. These compelling stories will showcase the diverse range of products that have been transformed through effective flipping strategies. We will explore how individuals have capitalized on market gaps, identified high-demand items, and implemented creative refurbishments to achieve remarkable returns on their investments. Each case study will offer a unique perspective, shedding light on the challenges faced, pivotal decisions made, and the ultimate triumph of turning a passion for flipping goods into a thriving business. From vintage furniture restoration to upcycling electronics, these stories will exemplify the power of innovation and determination in the world of flipping. Readers will gain firsthand knowledge of the practical considerations, such as pricing negotiations, target audience engagement, and the cultivation of a loyal customer base. By immersing ourselves in these case studies, we can extract valuable lessons, guiding principles, and success-driven methodologies that are transferable to any flipping endeavor, regardless of the industry or niche. Moreover, by analyzing these real-world examples, readers will be inspired to visualize their own potential within the domain of flipping, fostering an entrepreneurial mindset and a keen eye for opportunity. The culmination of these case studies will provide a comprehensive understanding of the intricacies involved in orchestrating a successful flipping enterprise, reaffirming that with dedication, resilience, and strategic acumen, the prospect of substantial financial reward is within reach.

Scaling Operations: Turning a Side Hustle into a Full-Fledged Venture

As you've delved into the world of flipping goods, honed your skills, and built up a successful track record, the next step is to scale your operations and transition from a side hustle to a full-fledged venture. Scaling a business involves carefully expanding its size and scope while maintaining quality and profitability. Here are several key strategies for scaling your flipping operation effectively. Firstly, consider the potential for automation and systemization. As your business grows, it becomes increasingly important to streamline processes to handle larger volumes of transactions. Implementing systems that can automate certain aspects of sourcing, repairing, and selling products can help increase efficiency and save time, allowing you to focus on strategic decision-making and growth initiatives. Secondly, establishing strategic partnerships can significantly contribute to scalability. Collaborating with reliable suppliers, repair workshops, or logistics companies can streamline the sourcing and restoration process, ensuring a consistent supply of high-quality goods to meet increasing demand. Additionally, forming strategic alliances with complementary businesses can extend your reach and customer base, providing opportunities for mutual promotion and growth. Thirdly, developing a strong brand identity and customer loyalty program is crucial when scaling operations. Building a reputable and recognizable brand can help differentiate your products in the market and create a loyal customer base that continues to support your growing business. Implementing a customer loyalty program to reward repeat buyers can further incentivize continued patronage and referrals. Another essential consideration when scaling your business is the utilization of data and analytics for informed decision-making. Employing robust reporting and analytics tools can provide valuable insights into customer behavior, market trends, and operational performance, guiding strategic expansion and optimization of your business. Utilize this information to make informed decisions about inventory management, pricing strategies, and targeted marketing efforts. Finally, don't overlook the importance of hiring and training the right talent. As your business grows, having skilled and dedicated personnel becomes pivotal to maintaining quality and efficiency. Invest in recruiting individuals who align with your business values and provide comprehensive training to ensure they understand and uphold your standards. Empower your team to take ownership of their roles and contribute to the overall success of the venture. By strategically implementing these scaling strategies, you can successfully evolve your flipping side hustle into a thriving, full-fledged venture positioned for sustained growth and success.

Ways To Make Extra Income

Pet Ventures: Profitable Paw-sibilities in Dog Walking

Introduction to Pet Ventures: Exploring the Market Landscape

The pet industry has experienced a significant upsurge in recent years, reflecting shifting societal attitudes towards pets as valued members of the family. Within this industry, the demand for professional pet services, particularly dog walking, has escalated in tandem with the rising number of dual-income households and urban dwellers. Understanding the market dynamics within the dog walking industry is crucial for aspiring entrepreneurs seeking to capitalize on this burgeoning demand. As more individuals embrace pet ownership, the need for reliable, professional dog walking services becomes increasingly pronounced. This heightened demand presents a unique opportunity for business-minded individuals to establish thriving ventures in the pet care sector. The market landscape within the dog walking industry encompasses a diverse range of potential clients, including busy professionals, elderly individuals, and individuals with physical limitations. Moreover, the emphasis on pet wellness and the inclination towards outsourcing pet care activities further contribute to the expansion of this market. Entrepreneurs delving into the realm of dog walking must recognize the multifaceted nature of this industry, addressing not only the physical exercise needs of pets but also their social and emotional well-being. By exploring the market landscape, individuals can gain valuable insights into the preferences and expectations of pet owners, allowing them to tailor their services to meet these needs effectively. Additionally, understanding the competitive landscape, regional variations in demand, and the evolving trends within the pet care industry are pivotal in formulating a successful business strategy. Finally, aspiring dog walking entrepreneurs should consider the integration of technology and digital platforms to streamline operations, enhance client communication, and distinguish their services amidst a competitive market. With a comprehensive exploration of the market landscape, entrepreneurs can position themselves strategically within the dog walking industry, leveraging opportunities and mitigating challenges to cultivate thriving and sustainable pet ventures.

The Business of Dog Walking: Opportunities and Challenges

As with any entrepreneurial venture, the dog walking business presents a myriad of opportunities and challenges. On the one hand, the increasing number of pet owners in urban areas provides a substantial market for dog walking services. The demand for convenient and reliable pet care solutions continues to grow, creating ample opportunities for individuals looking to capitalize on this trend. Moreover, as more people opt for pet ownership, there is a corresponding need for professional dog walkers to cater to their pets' exercise and socialization needs. This burgeoning demand provides a fertile landscape for aspiring dog walking entrepreneurs to establish thriving businesses. However, amid these promising prospects, it's crucial to recognize and navigate the challenges inherent in this industry. One of the primary challenges dog walkers face is managing unpredictable schedules, as the nature of the job often entails accommodating clients' varying time constraints. Additionally, inclement weather conditions can pose significant obstacles, affecting both the dogs' willingness to go outdoors and the reliability of transportation. Furthermore, ensuring the safety and well-being of the dogs under one's care is paramount, necessitating a high level of responsibility and attentiveness at all times. As a dog walker, overcoming such challenges requires a blend of adaptability, organization, and a genuine passion for working with animals. Developing a thorough understanding of the nuances within the business, including client expectations and canine behavior, is pivotal to navigating the unique challenges while embracing the rewarding opportunities that come with the profession.

Credentialing and Training: Establishing Expertise

As a professional in the pet ventures industry, acquiring the necessary credentials and training is paramount to positioning yourself as an expert dog walker. This section delves into the various avenues through which individuals can establish their expertise in this field. One of the fundamental steps in credentialing is obtaining certifications from recognized organizations such as the National Association of Professional Pet Sitters (NAPPS) or Pet Sitters International (PSI). These certifications not only lend credibility to your skill set but also assure potential clients of your commitment to excellence in pet care. In addition to formal certifications, investing in specialized training programs that focus on dog behavior, first aid, and emergency protocols is pivotal for honing your expertise. Several reputable institutions and online platforms offer comprehensive courses that cover these essential aspects, empowering you to handle a diverse range of canine needs with confidence and competence. Furthermore, pursuing continuous education through workshops, seminars, and conferences within the pet care industry fosters a proactive approach to staying abreast of the latest trends and best practices. It also provides invaluable networking opportunities with fellow professionals. Apart from credentials and training, nurturing expertise as a dog walker involves gaining hands-on experience. Volunteering at animal shelters, interning with established pet care businesses, or apprenticing under seasoned dog walkers are viable means of acquiring practical skills and insights. Building a robust portfolio of experiences not only enhances your proficiency but also instills trust and reliability among prospective clients. Lastly, establishing expertise extends to cultivating a strong understanding of local regulations and laws pertaining to pet care services.

Familiarizing yourself with licensing requirements, liability issues, and insurance obligations is crucial for safeguarding your business against potential legal pitfalls. By navigating these facets with diligence, dedication, and a commitment to ongoing learning, you can forge a reputation as a trusted and knowledgeable professional in the thriving realm of dog walking and pet ventures.

Legal and Insurance Considerations: Protecting Your Business

As you delve deeper into the realm of pet ventures, particularly in the domain of dog walking, it becomes imperative to address the critical aspect of legal and insurance considerations. Protecting your business from potential liabilities and unforeseen circumstances is fundamental to its sustainability and growth. Here, we will explore the various dimensions of safeguarding your enterprise through prudent legal and insurance measures.

First and foremost, it is essential to establish your business as a legal entity. Whether you opt for a sole proprietorship, limited liability company (LLC), or another suitable structure, formalizing your business not only instills credibility but also provides a distinct separation between personal and business assets, shielding you from personal liability in the event of legal issues or financial debts.

In conjunction with legal structuring, securing comprehensive business insurance is paramount. A tailored insurance policy specifically designed for pet-related services, such as dog walking, can offer protection against third-party claims arising from property damage, injury, or negligence. Additionally, consider augmenting your coverage with bonding, which inspires confidence in potential clients by assuring them that your business is financially secure and trustworthy.

Furthermore, navigating the legal landscape necessitates a thorough understanding of local regulations and ordinances pertaining to pet care businesses, including licensing requirements, zoning restrictions, and animal welfare laws. Compliance with these regulations is non-negotiable and underscores your commitment to ethical and responsible business practices.

In parallel, drafting meticulously crafted service agreements and liability waivers is crucial in delineating the terms of engagement with your clients and mitigating potential disputes. An attorney well-versed in business law can provide invaluable assistance in customizing these legal documents to align with the specific nuances of your dog walking operation.

Lastly, amidst the intricacies of legal and insurance considerations, seek professional counsel from legal advisors and insurance experts who specialize in the pet industry. Their insights and expertise can elucidate nuanced aspects of risk management and ensure that your business is fortified with robust legal protections and adequate insurance coverage.

In this dynamic and evolving landscape, safeguarding your dog walking venture through stringent legal compliance and comprehensive insurance safeguards is indispensable for fostering trust, reliability, and sustainable growth within the competitive pet care market.

Building Clientele: Marketing Strategies for Success

To thrive in the competitive world of pet ventures, particularly in the realm of dog walking, mastering marketing strategies is essential to attract and retain clientele. Effective marketing encompasses a multifaceted approach that not only promotes your services but also establishes a strong brand presence within the community. One fundamental strategy for building clientele is to leverage digital platforms and social media channels. Create captivating content showcasing your expertise, testimonials from satisfied clients, and engaging posts that highlight the joys and benefits of responsible pet ownership. Utilize targeted advertising on platforms such as Facebook, Instagram, and local community forums to reach potential customers. Additionally, maintain an informative and visually appealing website that conveys professionalism and instills confidence in prospective clients. Beyond digital outreach, networking within the local pet owner community and collaborating with veterinarians, groomers, and pet stores can greatly enhance your visibility and credibility. Establishing partnerships with these stakeholders not only expands your referral network but also reinforces your reputation as a trusted and reliable pet care provider. Offering promotional events, discounts, or referral incentives can incentivize existing clients to spread the word about your exceptional services. Another vital aspect of building clientele is delivering exceptional service that fosters client loyalty and positive word-of-mouth referrals. Prioritize clear communication, reliability, and attentiveness to each pet's needs, ensuring a personalized and memorable experience for both the pets and their owners. Requesting and showcasing client testimonials and reviews prominently on your marketing materials and online platforms can further bolster your credibility and attract new clients. Continuously seek feedback and stay adaptable to evolving client preferences and industry trends. By implementing a well-rounded marketing approach that combines digital outreach, community engagement, and superior service delivery, aspiring dog-walking entrepreneurs can effectively build a loyal clientele and establish a reputable presence in the flourishing pet care industry.

Setting Rates and Pricing Strategies: Maximizing Profitability

Setting competitive rates and implementing effective pricing strategies are imperative for maximizing profitability in the dog walking business. The key to establishing rates lies in striking a balance between offering competitive prices that appeal to prospective clients while ensuring that your services remain financially sustainable. Achieving this balance requires thorough market research to understand the prevailing rates in your area, as well as an appreciation for the unique value that you bring to the table. Consider factors such as the duration of walks, additional services offered (e.g., feeding, grooming), and the number of dogs walked simultaneously. When setting rates, it's essential to convey the quality of service that sets you apart from competitors, reassuring clients that they are receiving exceptional value for their investment. Additionally, flexible pricing options, such as discounted monthly packages or referral rewards, can incentivize client retention and generate word-of-mouth referrals. Emphasizing transparency in pricing not only fosters trust with clients but also demonstrates professionalism and integrity in business operations. Business costs, including insurance, transportation, and supplies, should be factored into the pricing model to ensure profitability. Regularly reassessing pricing strategies based on client feedback, market trends, and the evolving needs of pet owners is crucial for staying competitive and adapting to changes in the industry landscape. By consistently refining your pricing strategies and maintaining a deep understanding of your target market, you can position your dog walking business for sustained profitability and long-term success.

Tools of the Trade: Equipment Essentials for Dog Walkers

A successful dog walking business relies heavily on having the right tools and equipment to ensure a safe, enjoyable, and productive experience for both the walker and the dogs. The proper equipment not only enhances the overall quality of service but also contributes to the safety and well-being of the dogs in your care. As a professional dog walker, investing in high-quality equipment is non-negotiable.

One of the most essential pieces of equipment for any dog walker is, undoubtedly, a reliable and sturdy leash. A leash not only serves as a means of control but also ensures the safety of the dogs under your supervision. Opt for a leash made from durable materials that can withstand different weather conditions and the pulling force of larger dogs. Additionally, consider investing in leashes of varying lengths to accommodate different breeds and walking environments.

Collars or harnesses are equally important for ensuring the comfort and security of the dogs. Selecting the appropriate collar or harness based on the size, breed, and behavior of each dog is vital. Adjustable and well-padded collars or harnesses help in preventing any discomfort or chafing during walks.

Another indispensable tool is waste management and disposal supplies. Being a responsible walker involves cleaning up after the dogs. Arm yourself with biodegradable waste bags and a sturdy pooper scooper to maintain cleanliness and hygiene while out on walks.

Furthermore, a first aid kit tailored specifically for dogs is essential for every professional dog walker. This kit should include basic medical supplies such as bandages, antiseptic wipes, tweezers, and any other necessary items to address minor injuries or emergencies.

Prioritize the safety and well-being of the dogs by being prepared for unexpected situations.

Comfortable and supportive footwear is crucial for a dog walker who spends extensive time on their feet. Invest in shoes that provide adequate support, traction, and durability to minimize the risk of foot and ankle-related injuries during long walks. Similarly, weather-appropriate clothing and accessories, such as waterproof gear and sun protection, are imperative to ensure comfort and safety regardless of the environmental conditions.

In addition to these fundamental tools, implementing technology solutions like GPS tracking devices and mobile communication devices can enhance the efficiency of the dog walking business. These tools offer added security and enable effective communication with clients in real-time, fostering trust and confidence in your services.

Equipping yourself with the right tools not only elevates the professionalism of your dog walking business but also demonstrates your commitment to providing the best possible care for the dogs entrusted to you.

Managing Time Effectively: Scheduling and Client Management

As a professional in the pet ventures industry, effective time management is paramount to success. Scheduling and client management are crucial components that can make or break your dog walking business. This section will delve into the strategies and practices essential for seamlessly organizing your schedule and effectively managing your clients.

The first step in managing time effectively is to implement a reliable scheduling system. Utilizing digital tools and applications designed for appointment management can streamline the process. Consider investing in scheduling software that allows clients to book and manage appointments online, thus reducing administrative tasks and ensuring accuracy in scheduling. Additionally, adopting a digital calendar that syncs across devices can help you stay organized and on top of your appointments.

Client management is equally important in maintaining a successful dog walking business. Building and nurturing strong relationships with your clients is key to long-term success. Prompt and clear communication is vital. Establishing efficient channels for communication, such as email, text messaging, or a dedicated client portal, ensures that you can quickly address any client inquiries or concerns. Moreover, maintaining an up-to-date client database with detailed notes regarding each pet's specific needs and preferences demonstrates professionalism and attentiveness, fostering trust and loyalty among your clientele.

When scheduling appointments, it's crucial to factor in travel time between locations to avoid any overlap or lateness. A well-planned route optimized for efficiency can prevent unnecessary stress and potential disruptions to your service. Furthermore, setting realistic timeframes for each appointment while considering unforeseen circumstances, such as traffic or inclement weather, is pivotal in providing reliable and consistent service.

In terms of client management, establishing transparent policies and procedures from the onset can help manage expectations and mitigate potential conflicts. Clearly outlining your services, rates, cancellation policies, and any additional charges ensures that both you and your clients are aligned on the terms of engagement. Moreover, implementing efficient invoicing and payment systems can contribute to a seamless client management process, allowing for timely and hassle-free transactions.

By mastering the art of scheduling and client management, you can ensure that your dog walking business operates smoothly and professionally. These essential practices not only enhance the overall customer experience but also optimize your operational efficiency, setting the stage for sustainable growth and success in the pet ventures industry.

Expanding Services: Beyond Basic Dog Walking

As a dog walker aspiring to advance in the pet care industry, it is essential to expand services beyond basic dog walking. By offering additional services, such as pet sitting, grooming, training, and even incorporating technology-driven solutions like fitness tracking and customized meal planning, you can create a comprehensive and appealing pet care package for your clients. Providing these supplementary services not only enhances the value proposition for your business but also provides added convenience and peace of mind for pet owners.

Diversifying your offerings also opens up new revenue streams and broadens your client base by catering to a wider range of pet care needs. For example, incorporating pet-first aid and CPR training can attract pet owners who prioritize safety and well-being. Additionally, exploring partnerships with local veterinarians, pet stores, and grooming salons can further enrich your service portfolio and establish you as a one-stop solution for pet care needs in your community.

Efficiently managing expanded services requires careful consideration of logistics and resources. Developing standardized procedures for each service, setting clear expectations with clients, and ensuring adequate staffing or outsourcing when necessary are crucial aspects to master. Comprehensive training for yourself and any employees in these extended services is paramount to maintaining quality and credibility.

Furthermore, as you expand your services, it becomes imperative to leverage technology for streamlined operations. Utilizing scheduling software, customer relationship management (CRM) systems, and digital marketing tools can optimize workflow, improve client communication, and enhance overall professionalism. Embracing technology not only facilitates efficient service delivery but also demonstrates a commitment to staying current and competitive in the evolving pet care landscape.

Finally, expanding services creates an opportunity to cultivate deeper connections within the pet care community. Engaging in collaborations and knowledge-sharing with other pet care professionals can lead to valuable insights, referrals, and potential partnerships. Attending industry events, conferences, and networking opportunities can also provide exposure to emerging trends and best practices, further empowering you to navigate your expanding service offerings with expertise.

In summary, venturing beyond basic dog walking through diversified service offerings presents a myriad of benefits, including increased revenue, a broader clientele, improved operational efficiency, and enriched professional relationships. Strategically expanding your pet care services equips you to stay at the forefront of the industry, setting a high standard for excellence and innovation.

Real-Life Success Stories: Lessons from Industry Leaders

In the realm of pet ventures and dog walking businesses, success stories from industry leaders offer invaluable insights and inspiration for budding entrepreneurs. These stories not only serve as testaments to the viability of such ventures but also shed light on the strategies, challenges, and triumphs encountered along the way. One such exemplary tale is that of Sarah Parker, a trailblazer in the dog walking industry. Sarah started her business, 'Paws R Us,' with a profound love for dogs and an unwavering commitment to providing exceptional care. Through relentless dedication and a keen understanding of customer needs, Sarah expanded her services beyond traditional dog walking, offering specialized training, grooming, and pet sitting. This diversification not only set 'Paws R Us' apart from competitors but also created additional revenue streams. By leveraging social media and local networks, Sarah effectively marketed her business, fostering strong relationships with both human clients and their furry companions. Sarah's ability to turn her passion into profit serves as an inspiring lesson for aspiring entrepreneurs. Another noteworthy success story is that of Max Johnson, who transformed his love for pets into a thriving dog walking business, 'Happy Tails.' By focusing on personalized, attentive service, Max established a loyal clientele base that became the cornerstone of his success. To scale his business, Max employed technology to streamline scheduling, billing, and client communication, enabling him to accommodate a growing demand without compromising quality. By diversifying his services to include pet transportation and customized exercise programs, Max solidified 'Happy Tails' as a comprehensive pet care provider in his community. Both Sarah and Max demonstrate the importance of innovation, adaptability, and unwavering dedication in building successful pet ventures. Their journeys exemplify the transformative potential inherent in pursuing a business centered around one's passion for animals. The unique paths taken by these industry leaders offer valuable lessons that can guide aspiring entrepreneurs in navigating the competitive landscape of pet-related ventures and dog walking businesses.

Ways To Make Extra Income

Launching Your Own Product: From Idea to Execution

Identifying Market Opportunities

In today's dynamic business landscape, identifying market opportunities is crucial for entrepreneurs and business owners. Recognizing emerging market trends and unmet consumer needs is the foundation for successful product development and business growth. Discovering ways to spot these opportunities involves a deep understanding of consumer behavior, industry trends, and competitive landscapes. Conducting market research, analyzing data, and observing patterns are fundamental steps in this process. Furthermore, staying abreast of societal changes, technological advancements, and cultural shifts allows astute entrepreneurs to identify gaps in the market that present lucrative business prospects.

Spotting emerging market trends requires a proactive approach to monitoring various industry sectors and consumer behaviors. By staying informed about the latest developments and evolving preferences, entrepreneurs can anticipate shifts in demand and capitalize on emerging opportunities. Utilizing both qualitative and quantitative research methods, such as surveys, focus groups, and data analysis, aids in understanding consumer needs and preferences. Additionally, engaging in trend forecasting and scenario planning enables entrepreneurs to predict potential market developments and adapt their strategies accordingly.

Uncovering unmet consumer needs involves empathizing with the target audience and recognizing pain points or inefficiencies in existing products or services. This necessitates direct interaction and engagement with consumers through feedback collection, interviews, and observation. By actively listening to consumer insights and identifying areas of dissatisfaction or unaddressed needs, entrepreneurs can innovate and develop solutions that cater to these underserved market segments. Moreover, leveraging tools such as social listening and trend analysis helps in discerning emerging conversations and sentiments within specific consumer segments, providing valuable indications for new market opportunities.

Ultimately, seizing market opportunities requires a well-informed and open-minded approach that integrates insights from diverse sources. By constantly evaluating industry shifts, consumer behaviors, and unmet needs, entrepreneurs can position themselves at the forefront of innovation and capitalize on untapped market spaces.

Conducting Comprehensive Market Research

As you embark on the journey of launching your own product, conducting comprehensive market research is a crucial step in understanding the landscape in which your product will exist. Market research involves gathering and analyzing information about consumer preferences, market trends, competitor strategies, and industry dynamics to make informed decisions. To begin with, it is imperative to identify the target demographic for your product. This entails studying the age, gender, location, income level, and psychographic traits of potential consumers. By segmenting the market based on these factors, you can tailor your product to meet the specific needs and desires of your intended audience. Furthermore, delving into market trends and consumer behavior patterns provides valuable insights into evolving preferences and purchasing habits. Understanding the competitive landscape is equally essential. Analyze competitors' products, pricing strategies, distribution channels, and marketing tactics to identify gaps and opportunities within the market. Concurrently, examining industry regulations and economic factors that may impact your product's success is integral. Market research methods include both primary and secondary research. Primary research involves collecting data firsthand through surveys, interviews, focus groups, and observations. On the other hand, secondary research utilizes existing sources such as industry reports, government publications, and academic studies to gather relevant information. Combining both approaches equips you with a comprehensive understanding of the market. Once data has been gathered, analysis becomes paramount. Utilize statistical tools and qualitative analysis techniques to interpret the collected information, identify patterns, and draw meaningful conclusions. The findings from market research will aid in making informed decisions at various stages of product development and promotion, ranging from design and features to pricing and branding strategies. A thorough market research process not only minimizes risks but also maximizes opportunities by ensuring that your product aligns with consumer demand and preferences. Ultimately, a well-researched product stands a greater chance of resonating with the target market and achieving sustainable success in the competitive business landscape.

Designing a Unique and Viable Product

In the quest to launch a successful product, designing a unique and viable offering is crucial. A well-conceived product holds the power to captivate target audiences and carve out a distinct niche in the market. To achieve this, it's imperative to start by deeply understanding the pain points and unmet needs of the intended customer base. By conducting thorough research and gathering insights, one can identify opportunities for innovation and differentiation. With a clear understanding of the competitive landscape, it becomes possible to brainstorm and conceptualize a product that not only addresses existing shortcomings but also has a compelling value proposition.

The process of ensuring the uniqueness and viability of a product involves meticulous attention to design and functionality. This encompasses not only the physical attributes but also the user experience and interface. Every aspect, from aesthetics to usability, must be crafted to resonate with the target audience. Engaging in iterative prototyping and testing allows for refining the product to meet or exceed customer expectations.

Moreover, sustainability and ethical considerations are increasingly becoming pivotal factors in product design. Integrating eco-friendly materials and practices not only aligns with contemporary consumer values but also positions the product favorably in the market. Ensuring that the product's life cycle and impact on the environment are conscientiously considered can enhance its appeal and long-term viability.

Additionally, embracing technological advancements can greatly contribute to making the product stand out. Incorporating cutting-edge features or leveraging advancements in manufacturing processes can elevate the product's desirability and value proposition. Furthermore, exploring avenues for customization and personalization can empower consumers to have a more intimate and tailored experience with the product, fostering stronger loyalty and satisfaction.

Ultimately, designing a unique and viable product demands an unwavering commitment to quality and innovation. It necessitates a holistic approach that takes into account market dynamics, consumer insights, design principles, and sustainable practices. By embodying these principles, one can create a product that not only fulfills unmet needs but also inspires and delights its audience, laying a solid foundation for success in the marketplace.

Developing a Solid Business Plan

A solid business plan serves as the roadmap for your entrepreneurial journey, providing a detailed framework for achieving success and sustainability. This crucial document outlines your business concept, market analysis, competitive landscape, marketing and sales strategy, operations, management structure, and financial projections. It not only helps you clarify your vision but also acts as a tool to secure funding, attract partners, and measure progress. When developing your business plan, begin with a comprehensive executive summary that encapsulates the essence of your venture. Next, delve into a thorough description of your company, its mission, vision, and values, along with an analysis of the target market, customer segments, and competitive positioning. In the marketing and sales section, outline your go-to-market strategy, pricing, promotion, and distribution channels, demonstrating a clear understanding of your approach to acquiring and retaining customers. Operations and management details should cover the organizational structure, staffing plan, and day-to-day workflow, showcasing your ability to execute the business idea efficiently and sustainably. However, the financial projections are crucial, including revenue forecasts, expenses, break-even analysis, and potential sources of funding. Furthermore, consider future scalability, risks, and exit strategies, displaying a long-term perspective and adaptability. To develop a solid business plan, research extensively, gather accurate data, validate assumptions, and seek professional guidance if necessary. An effective business plan is not just a static document; it should be viewed as a dynamic tool that evolves alongside your business, guiding decision-making and adaptation in response to market feedback and changing conditions. As such, revisit and refine your business plan regularly, ensuring that it remains aligned with your objectives and market realities. Ultimately, a well-crafted business plan is the foundation on which you can build a successful and sustainable enterprise, guiding your actions, attracting stakeholders, and steering your business towards growth and profitability.

Securing Funding and Resources

Securing funding and resources is a critical step in the process of launching your own product. Without adequate financial backing and necessary resources, it can be challenging to bring your product from concept to market. This section will cover various methods and strategies for securing the essential funding and resources needed to drive your business forward. One of the primary avenues for securing funding is through traditional financing options such as small business loans, lines of credit, or venture capital. It's important to thoroughly research and understand the terms and conditions associated with each type of financing to make an informed decision that aligns with your business goals and financial capabilities.

Another effective approach for securing funding is by seeking out potential investors or partners who share an interest in your product or industry. This may involve pitching your business idea to angel investors, attending networking events, or leveraging online platforms designed to connect entrepreneurs with potential investors. A well-crafted pitch deck and business plan can significantly enhance your chances of securing investment from external sources.

In addition to monetary funding, identifying and acquiring the necessary resources for product development and production is crucial. This may involve establishing supplier relationships, sourcing raw materials, and setting up manufacturing facilities or production partners. Building a network of reliable suppliers and managing efficient supply chain logistics are vital components of ensuring a smooth and sustainable production process.

Furthermore, exploring alternative funding options, such as crowdfunding campaigns or grants, can provide innovative ways to secure initial capital while generating buzz and support for your product within the market. Engaging with the community and leveraging social media and digital platforms can amplify your reach and help generate momentum for your funding efforts.

It's important to carefully evaluate the overall financial needs of your business and create a detailed budget that encompasses all aspects of the product launch journey. This includes costs associated with research and development, prototyping, marketing, inventory management, and more. By diligently managing and allocating financial resources, you can position your business for long-term success and sustainability.

Ultimately, the process of securing funding and resources requires proactive diligence, strategic planning, and effective communication. By leveraging a combination of traditional financing, investor partnerships, resource procurement, and innovative funding avenues, you can lay a strong foundation for bringing your product to market and positioning your business for growth.

Establishing a Brand Identity

Establishing a compelling brand identity is crucial for differentiating your product in a competitive market and creating a lasting impression on consumers. A distinctive brand identity embodies the core values, mission, and vision of your business, portraying them in a visually and emotionally appealing manner that resonates with your target audience. The process of developing a brand identity involves comprehensive strategic planning and creative execution to ensure that it aligns seamlessly with your product and its intended positioning. Begin by conducting thorough market research and analyzing consumer insights to understand their preferences, pain points, and aspirations. This knowledge will serve as the foundation for crafting a brand identity that effectively connects with your potential customers, nurturing trust and loyalty. The next step is to define your brand's personality, voice, and visual elements, including logo design, color palette, typography, and imagery. These components should collectively convey the essence and character of your brand, evoking the desired emotional response and maintaining consistency across all touchpoints. Communicating your brand identity through various channels, such as packaging, marketing materials, website, and social media, allows you to reinforce a cohesive and memorable brand experience. It's essential to consider how your brand will be perceived in the marketplace and how it will differentiate itself from competitors, pinpointing unique selling propositions that resonate with your target market. Moreover, staying true to your brand's values and promises is pivotal in cultivating authenticity and building credibility. Crafting a compelling brand story that articulates the journey, purpose, and impact of your product can create an emotional connection with consumers, enhancing brand recall and affinity. Leveraging storytelling as a powerful tool to convey the essence of your brand can elevate its perception and establish a deeper connection with your audience. In conclusion, establishing a strong and resonant brand identity requires a blend of research, creativity, strategy, and consistency, culminating in a distinct and memorable representation of your product in the marketplace.

Prototyping and Testing

Prototyping and testing are crucial phases in the product development process as they allow for refinement and improvement before mass production. The prototyping stage involves creating a preliminary version of the product, often using 3D printing or other rapid prototyping techniques, to visualize its form and functionality. This step facilitates hands-on assessment and provides an opportunity to make necessary adjustments to the design. By creating prototypes, entrepreneurs can gather valuable feedback from potential users or focus groups, enabling them to address any shortcomings before finalizing the product.

Once the prototype has been developed, rigorous testing procedures are initiated to evaluate the product's performance, durability, and user experience. Testing may involve simulated usage scenarios, stress tests, and quality assurance checks to ensure that the product meets industry standards and customer expectations. Feedback from test results is meticulously analyzed to identify areas for improvement, whether in materials, construction, or usability.

In addition to functional testing, it is paramount to conduct market testing to gauge consumer response and gather insights into potential demand. This involves presenting the prototype to target consumers and obtaining their feedback through surveys, interviews, and observational studies. By understanding how the product resonates with the intended audience, entrepreneurs can fine-tune their offering to align more closely with customer preferences and needs.

Successfully navigating the prototyping and testing phase requires attention to detail, flexibility, and open-mindedness. It is important to approach this stage with a mindset geared towards continuous improvement and innovation. Entrepreneurs should be prepared to iterate on their designs based on feedback, and embrace the iterative nature of prototyping to achieve optimal results. Through effective prototyping and meticulous testing, entrepreneurs can mitigate risks associated with launching a flawed product, ultimately positioning themselves for success in the competitive market landscape.

Strategizing Production and Supply Chain Management

In the journey of bringing a product to market, one of the critical aspects revolves around strategizing production and supply chain management. A well-thought-out strategy in these areas can make or break the success of a product launch. Production and supply chain management involve the planning and coordination of activities required to turn raw materials into finished products and facilitate their distribution to end consumers. It encompasses a series of interconnected steps that demand careful consideration and meticulous execution.

When it comes to production, finding reliable and efficient manufacturing partners is paramount. Whether working with local factories or outsourcing to overseas suppliers, it's essential to prioritize factors such as quality control, production capacity, and adherence to ethical and environmental standards. Managing these relationships effectively is crucial for ensuring timely and cost-effective production.

Furthermore, supply chain management involves optimizing the flow of goods from the point of origin to the point of consumption. This often includes activities such as procurement, logistics, inventory management, and distribution. Efficiency in supply chain management can result in reduced costs, improved customer satisfaction, and increased overall competitiveness.

Strategic sourcing plays a pivotal role in supply chain management. This involves identifying and selecting suppliers based on various criteria, such as reliability, cost, and responsiveness. Choosing the right suppliers can lead to enhanced quality, better pricing, and minimized supply chain disruptions.

Another crucial element is demand forecasting, which helps in predicting future demand for the product. Accurate demand forecasting enables effective inventory management, reducing the risk of stockouts or excess inventory. Utilizing technology and analytics can aid in generating more precise demand forecasts, thereby streamlining production and minimizing waste.

Moreover, embracing lean manufacturing principles can significantly enhance production efficiency. Lean practices focus on eliminating waste and optimizing processes, ultimately leading to improved productivity, reduced lead times, and lower production costs. Implementing lean techniques requires a deep understanding of the entire production process and constant commitment to continuous improvement.

To optimize supply chain management, integrating advanced technologies such as RFID, IoT, and cloud-based systems can provide real-time visibility into the movement of goods, enhance inventory tracking, and improve collaboration with suppliers. Leveraging data analytics can also offer valuable insights for enhancing operational efficiency and making informed decisions throughout the supply chain.

Ultimately, effective strategic planning in production and supply chain management demands an integrated approach, meticulous attention to detail, and the ability to adapt to dynamic market conditions. By focusing on efficiency, quality, and innovation, businesses can navigate the complexities of production and supply chain management while positioning themselves for long-term success.

Implementing Effective Marketing Strategies

To ensure the success of your product launch, implementing effective marketing strategies is paramount. Marketing serves as the bridge between your product and your target audience, making it crucial to design and execute a comprehensive plan that resonates with potential customers. Here's how you can approach this vital aspect.

Firstly, identify your target market segments and understand their demographics, preferences, and behaviors. This will enable you to tailor your marketing efforts and messages more effectively. Utilize data analytics and market research to gain insights into consumer trends and purchasing patterns, allowing you to make informed decisions.

Next, craft a compelling brand story that communicates the value proposition of your product. Emphasize what sets your offering apart from competitors and how it addresses specific pain points or desires of your target audience. Establishing a strong brand identity fosters trust and credibility, laying a solid foundation for customer engagement.

Leverage multi-channel marketing approaches to reach a wider audience. Utilize social media platforms, email marketing, content marketing, and search engine optimization (SEO) to create an integrated campaign that maximizes visibility and engagement. Consistency across various marketing channels reinforces brand recognition and amplifies your message.

Engage in influencer partnerships and collaborations to extend your reach and tap into established networks. Identify influencers whose followers align with your target demographic and forge authentic relationships. Their endorsements and testimonials carry weight with their audiences, lending credibility and exposure to your product.

Additionally, consider leveraging user-generated content. Encourage satisfied customers to share their experiences with your product on social media, fostering a sense of community and authenticity around your brand. User-generated content serves as powerful social proof, influencing potential buyers and building brand advocacy.

Furthermore, analyze and optimize your marketing campaigns through A/B testing and performance metrics. Continually assess the effectiveness of different strategies and channels, refining your approach based on real-time data. This iterative process allows you to allocate resources efficiently and maximize return on investment.

Lastly, consider the timing and cadence of your marketing initiatives. Coordinate product launches and promotional efforts with peak consumer periods or industry events to capitalize on heightened consumer interest and attention. Strategic timing can amplify the impact of your marketing activities, driving awareness and sales.

By implementing these marketing strategies thoughtfully and methodically, you can effectively position your product in the marketplace, generate demand, and drive sustained growth.

Evaluating Performance and Scaling Operations

As a savvy entrepreneur, the ability to evaluate the performance of your product and scale operations is crucial for long-term success. Once your product has been launched into the market, it is essential to constantly monitor its performance and gather insights to inform your scaling strategies. One key aspect of evaluating performance is analyzing sales data, customer feedback, and market trends to identify areas for improvement and growth opportunities. Leveraging tools such as analytics software, customer surveys, and industry reports can provide valuable metrics to assess performance and guide strategic decision-making. By conducting regular reviews and analysis, you can gain a deeper understanding of consumer preferences, competitive dynamics, and operational efficiencies.

Scaling operations involves expanding your business in response to increased demand or market potential. This may include ramping up production, distribution, and marketing efforts to meet growing customer needs. It also involves optimizing internal processes to accommodate larger volumes while maintaining quality standards and cost-effectiveness. Moreover, scaling operations entails building strategic partnerships and strengthening supply chain capabilities to support the heightened demands of a growing business. Additionally, it requires implementing agile structures and systems that can adapt to changing market conditions and consumer behaviors.

To successfully scale operations, it is imperative to set clear objectives and develop a scalable business model that can flexibly accommodate growth without compromising quality and customer satisfaction. This may involve investing in technology upgrades, hiring additional staff, or expanding physical infrastructure to facilitate increased production and distribution. Furthermore, establishing robust performance metrics and Key Performance Indicators (KPIs) will enable you to measure the effectiveness of your scaling efforts and make informed adjustments as needed.

When scaling operations, maintaining a customer-centric focus is paramount. Anticipating customer needs and delivering exceptional experiences at every touchpoint are vital for sustainable growth. Listening to customer feedback, adapting products based on market trends, and providing responsive customer service will help build brand loyalty and drive repeat business. By continuously refining and enhancing your product offerings and operational capabilities, you can position your business for long-term success and competitiveness in the marketplace.

Ways To Make Extra Income

Become a Coach: Sharing Expertise for Earnings

Understanding the Coaching Landscape

The coaching landscape is a dynamic and ever-evolving sector driven by current trends and demands. At its core, coaching has metamorphosed from being merely an avenue for personal development to becoming a strategic tool with wide applications across various domains. In today's fast-paced and competitive world, professionals, entrepreneurs, and individuals seek coaching to hone their skills, enhance performance, and achieve specific goals. The rise of coaching as a profession has been fueled by the growing need for specialized guidance, personalized mentorship, and structured support in both personal and professional realms.Trends within the coaching industry have shown an increased focus on areas such as leadership development, executive coaching, career transition, wellness coaching, and business growth strategies. These specific niches have experienced heightened demand, reflecting the evolving needs of individuals and organizations alike. The ongoing digital transformation has also significantly impacted the coaching landscape, leading to the proliferation of online coaching platforms, virtual mentoring, and remote client engagement.As market dynamics and preferences continue to shift, the coaching industry has responded by embracing diversity in specialization. Coaches now cater to niche markets including health and fitness, mindfulness and well-being, entrepreneurship, productivity enhancement, and relationship management. Moreover, emerging trends in technology integration, artificial intelligence, and data-driven coaching methodologies are progressively reshaping the structure and delivery of coaching services, making it imperative for practitioners to stay abreast of these advancements. Industry leaders and stakeholders are also emphasizing the importance of ethical standards, credentialing, and regulatory compliance within the coaching profession, reinforcing the significance of maintaining quality and integrity in coaching practices.Ultimately, understanding the coaching landscape entails recognizing the multifaceted demands, trends, and specializations that shape the industry. By delving into these intricacies, aspiring coaches can position themselves effectively, adapt to market shifts, and tailor their expertise to meet the evolving needs of their clientele.This heightened appreciation for the industry's evolution cultivates a deeper understanding of the nuanced requirements and expectations from both the coach and coachee perspectives. It reinforces the need for continuous learning, adaptation, and proactive response to changing paradigms and paradigms, enabling coaching professionals to thrive and contribute meaningfully to the personal and professional growth journeys of their clients.

Identifying Your Niche and Expertise

When venturing into the coaching business, identifying your niche and expertise is crucial for establishing a strong foundation. Your niche is the specific area in which you will specialize and offer your services, while your expertise refers to the knowledge and skills you possess that provide value to your potential clients. Identifying the right niche and expertise involves a process of introspection, research, and careful consideration.

Begin by reflecting on your passions, strengths, and experiences. Consider the subjects or areas where you excel and derive genuine enjoyment. Look back on your professional journey and personal interests to pinpoint the intersection of what you love and what you're exceptionally good at. For instance, if you have a background in marketing and a passion for personal development, your niche could revolve around coaching entrepreneurs on branding and marketing strategies.

Conduct thorough market research to understand the demand and competition within your identified niche. Analyze the needs and challenges of your target audience, and assess how your expertise can address those pain points effectively. This step is essential in ensuring that there is a viable market for your coaching services and that your unique approach can carve out a distinctive space in the industry.

Furthermore, seek feedback from mentors, peers, or potential clients to gauge their perception of your expertise and the proposed niche. Their insights can provide valuable validation or reveal blind spots that require attention. Leveraging their perspectives can refine your understanding of not only your strengths but also the gaps in the market that your expertise can fill.

As you narrow down your niche and expertise, consider the long-term sustainability and growth opportunities within that segment. Is the niche broad enough to attract a sizable client base, yet specific enough to position you as an authority? Does your expertise align with the evolving trends and demands of the market? Evaluating these aspects will help you make an informed decision that lays the groundwork for a successful coaching practice.

Ultimately, the process of identifying your niche and expertise is a pivotal step that shapes your entire coaching venture. By investing time and effort into this stage, you can position yourself for relevance, credibility, and resonance within your chosen niche, setting the stage for impactful and rewarding engagements with your clients.

Setting Up a Coaching Business

Setting up a coaching business requires careful planning and strategic decision-making. This section will guide you through the essential steps to establish a successful coaching enterprise. The first crucial task is to define your business structure and conduct thorough research on legal and financial considerations. Decide whether to register as a sole proprietorship, partnership, or corporation after consulting with legal and financial advisors. Obtaining the necessary permits and licenses is also imperative to ensure compliance with local regulations. Establishing a clear business plan outlining your services, target market, and competitive analysis is fundamental. Analyze the demand for your coaching services, identifying your ideal clients, and conducting market research to understand the competition in your niche. Select a compelling and memorable business name that resonates with your brand and vision. After finalizing your business structure and plan, it's time to address operational aspects such as setting up a dedicated workspace, acquiring essential equipment, and implementing efficient administrative systems. Determining your pricing strategy involves assessing the value of your services, considering industry standards, and understanding your target audience's affordability. Building a professional online presence through a well-designed website, engaging social media profiles, and captivating branding materials is essential for attracting potential clients. Implement secure payment systems and establish clear terms of service to safeguard both parties' interests. Additionally, investing in robust client management tools and scheduling software will streamline client communication and appointment management. Prioritize building a network of contacts within the coaching industry and related fields to foster collaborations, referrals, and mentorship opportunities. Embrace continuous learning by seeking professional development opportunities, staying abreast of industry trends, and honing your coaching skills. Most importantly, embody integrity, empathy, and dedication in every aspect of your coaching business. As you navigate through the intricacies of setting up your coaching business, remember that patience, persistence, and adaptability are key virtues in reaching your entrepreneurial goals.

Developing a Coaching Curriculum

As a coach, developing a strong curriculum is crucial for delivering value and achieving lasting impact in your clients' lives. A well-structured coaching curriculum serves as the roadmap for your clients, guiding them through their learning and growth journey. When developing your coaching curriculum, it's important to begin by clearly defining your objectives and goals for the program. What specific outcomes do you aim to help your clients achieve? What skills, knowledge, or behavioral changes do you want them to develop? By having a clear understanding of your desired results, you can tailor your curriculum to directly address these targets. Effective coaching curriculums are built on a foundation of structured progression. Consider breaking down the overarching goals into smaller, manageable milestones. This allows for a sense of achievement at each stage and keeps clients motivated as they progress through the program. Furthermore, incorporating a variety of learning activities and materials into the curriculum helps cater to different learning styles and ensures a comprehensive approach to skill development. For instance, combining one-on-one coaching sessions with interactive workshops, reading assignments, and practical exercises can enhance the overall learning experience. It's also essential to continually evaluate and refine your coaching curriculum based on client feedback, market trends, and industry best practices. Flexibility and adaptability are key elements in ensuring that the curriculum remains relevant and impactful. Lastly, remember that a successful coaching curriculum not only imparts knowledge and skills but also inspires and empowers your clients. Incorporate elements that foster personal growth, self-reflection, and mindset shifts to create a transformative experience. By prioritizing these aspects, you can elevate the value of your coaching offering and position yourself as an influential guide in your clients' journey toward success.

Crafting Your Personal Brand

Crafting a compelling personal brand is essential for standing out in the coaching landscape. Your personal brand encompasses your values, strengths, expertise, and unique style, all of which contribute to your distinct identity as a coach. To begin, introspect on what sets you apart from other coaches. What unique experiences, skills, or perspectives do you bring to the table? Understanding your own story and the value you offer is crucial in defining your personal brand. Next, consider your target audience. What are their pain points, aspirations, and preferences? Tailoring your brand to resonate with your ideal clients can significantly enhance your appeal as a coach. A strong personal brand also involves consistency across various touchpoints. From your website and social media profiles to your coaching materials, ensure that your messaging, aesthetics, and voice align cohesively. This cultivates trust and familiarity among potential clients. Additionally, storytelling is a powerful tool in shaping your brand narrative. Authentically share your journey, successes, and even setbacks to create emotional connections with your audience. It humanizes your brand and builds relatability, fostering deeper engagement. Leveraging content marketing to showcase your expertise can elevate your personal brand. Blog posts, podcasts, webinars, and social media content not only demonstrate your knowledge but also reinforce your brand identity. Engage with your audience, address their concerns, and provide valuable insights to establish yourself as a reliable authority in your niche. Visual elements such as logos, color schemes, and imagery play a pivotal role in brand perception. Choose visuals that resonate with your brand's personality and speak to your target audience. Lastly, seek feedback from peers, mentors, and even potential clients. Constructive criticism and external perspectives can illuminate blind spots and refine your brand image. Continuous refinement is key as your coaching practice evolves. Crafting a compelling personal brand demands introspection, strategic positioning, and ongoing diligence, but the impact it has on establishing credibility and attracting clients is immeasurable.

Leveraging Digital Platforms for Reach

In today's digital age, the power of online platforms to expand your coaching business cannot be overstated. Leveraging digital platforms allows you to extend your reach far beyond geographical boundaries, connecting with potential clients globally. Social media platforms such as LinkedIn, Twitter, Facebook, and Instagram provide fertile ground for showcasing your expertise, sharing valuable content, and engaging with a diverse audience. By strategically utilizing these platforms, you can establish yourself as a thought leader in your niche, thereby attracting more clients and opportunities. Additionally, consider creating and sharing insightful articles, videos, and infographics on professional networks and industry-specific forums to further demonstrate your knowledge and expertise.
Furthermore, leveraging digital advertising on platforms like Google Ads or Facebook Ads can help target specific demographics, increasing the visibility of your coaching services. To maximize the impact of your digital presence, it's essential to maintain a consistent and authentic brand voice across all platforms. This ensures that your audience perceives a cohesive and compelling image of your coaching practice. As the digital landscape constantly evolves, staying updated on emerging platforms and trends is crucial. For instance, exploring the potential of podcasting, webinars, or even virtual reality experiences can set your coaching business apart and appeal to varied learning preferences.
Remember to monitor and analyze the performance of your digital initiatives using tools like Google Analytics or social media insights. Understanding what resonates with your online audience will enable you to refine your approach and optimize your digital strategy for maximum reach and engagement. Embracing digital platforms offers boundless opportunities for expanding your coaching practice, connecting with a diverse clientele, and establishing a lasting impact in your field.

Establishing Pricing and Packages

Establishing the right pricing and packages for your coaching services is a critical aspect of building a successful and sustainable coaching business. This process requires a thorough understanding of your target market, the value you offer, and industry standards. When determining your pricing strategy, it's important to consider the experience and expertise you bring to the table. Consider the time, effort, and resources devoted to honing your skills and knowledge, which directly contribute to the quality of service you provide to your clients. It's essential to strike a balance between offering competitive pricing and ensuring that the value you provide is reflected in your rates. Researching similar coaching services can offer insights into prevailing market rates, enabling you to position your offerings effectively. Additionally, think about the outcomes and transformations your coaching can bring to your clients' lives. Develop clear and transparent pricing packages that align with the specific needs of your target audience. Offer tiered options to cater to various budgets and requirements. By creating different packages, clients can choose the level of engagement and access to your services that best suits their needs. Each package should be tailored to deliver distinct benefits and solutions, presenting clients with a compelling range of choices. Discounts for long-term commitments or bundled services can incentivize clients to invest in extended coaching, strengthening your client base and revenue streams. Moreover, communicating the value and impact of each package will help clients understand the return on investment they can expect. Providing detailed breakdowns of the services included in each package can enhance transparency and build trust with potential clients. Building flexibility into your pricing structure allows for adjustments based on client feedback and changing market dynamics. It's crucial to remain adaptable and responsive to evolving client needs and industry trends. As your coaching practice grows, periodically reviewing and adjusting your pricing strategy will ensure that it remains aligned with the value you bring and the market demand. Continually reassess the competitive landscape and make proactive changes to stay ahead of the curve. Emphasize the transformative results of your coaching services and the long-term benefits of investing in personal development. Establishing an optimal pricing model and robust packages is fundamental to attracting and retaining high-value clientele, sustaining a profitable coaching business, and making a positive impact in the lives of your clients.

Building Client Relationships and Network

Developing and nurturing client relationships is paramount to a successful coaching practice. An effective coach-client relationship is built on empathy, trust, and communication. As a coach, it's crucial to understand your clients' needs, goals, and challenges on a personal level. This not only fosters trust but also allows for tailored guidance and support. Communication plays a pivotal role in this process, and active listening is key to comprehending your clients' concerns and aspirations.

Networking within professional circles is another essential aspect of building a strong client base. Engage with other professionals in related fields, attend industry events, and leverage social media platforms to connect with potential clients. Establishing credibility within the community and among peers is instrumental in attracting clientele. Additionally, seeking out mentorship from established coaches can provide valuable insights and opportunities for collaboration.

Maintaining transparency and professionalism in all interactions is vital. Clearly outlining the scope of services, discussing confidentiality measures, and setting realistic expectations contributes to a positive and sustainable rapport. Addressing feedback openly and adjusting coaching methods accordingly demonstrates commitment to client success. Furthermore, showcasing genuine care for your clients' progress beyond financial transactions cultivates long-term relationships.

A personalized approach in client relationship management sets exemplary coaches apart. Sending personalized messages on special occasions, providing additional resources tailored to individual needs, and offering occasional pro bono sessions as a token of appreciation can reinforce loyalty and trust. Remembering important milestones in clients' lives and career paths enhances the bond and showcases genuine investment in their well-being.

Networking strategies should encompass both online and offline efforts. Consistently maintaining a professional online presence through a robust website, engaging social media content, and regular blog posts or newsletters enhances visibility and credibility. In-person networking activities, such as hosting workshops, speaking engagements, and participating in industry panels, offer opportunities to connect with potential clients face-to-face and establish authority within the coaching realm.

In conclusion, cultivating strong client relationships and expanding professional networks are indispensable for the growth and sustainability of a coaching practice. Making meaningful connections, demonstrating genuine care, and maintaining professionalism are foundational principles that contribute to a thriving coaching business.

Scaling Your Coaching Practice

As your coaching practice gains traction and your client base expands, the need for scalability becomes increasingly apparent. Scaling your coaching business involves a strategic approach to accommodate growth while maintaining quality and value for your clients. One crucial aspect of scaling is to streamline your processes and operations. This may involve automating administrative tasks, leveraging technology for scheduling and communications, and implementing efficient client management systems. By optimizing these aspects, you can free up more time to focus on delivering high-quality coaching sessions and developing your expertise. Another vital component of scaling is to standardize your offerings and create a framework that allows for consistent delivery of your coaching services. Developing structured programs, toolkits, and resources can not only enhance the client experience but also facilitate easier replication and expansion of your coaching practice. Furthermore, consider the potential for collaboration and partnerships to broaden your reach and impact. This could involve teaming up with other coaches or professionals in complementary fields, forming strategic alliances, or even venturing into corporate coaching opportunities. Additionally, when scaling your coaching practice, it's essential to invest in continuous professional development. The field of coaching is ever-evolving, and staying updated with the latest methodologies, trends, and research is pivotal for maintaining relevance and authority in your niche. This might involve pursuing advanced certifications, attending industry events, or seeking mentorship from seasoned experts. Moreover, as your practice grows, don't underestimate the power of client feedback and testimonials. Positive reviews and success stories from satisfied clients can significantly contribute to your credibility and attract new clientele. Finally, scalability also entails prudent financial planning and resource allocation. As your coaching business expands, so do the demands on your time, energy, and finances. Developing a sustainable growth strategy, setting clear financial goals, and managing your resources effectively are paramount to ensure long-term success. By strategically scaling your coaching practice, you can unlock new opportunities, impact a wider audience, and achieve sustainable prosperity in the rapidly evolving landscape of coaching and personal development.

Measuring Success and Continuing Growth

As with any business endeavor, measuring the success of your coaching practice is essential for continued growth and improvement. There are several key metrics and strategies that can help you assess the performance of your coaching business and propel it to new heights. One of the most fundamental measures of success is client satisfaction and progress. Regularly evaluating client feedback and tracking their achievements will not only provide validation for your coaching methods but also highlight areas for refinement. Additionally, monitoring client retention rates can offer valuable insights into the effectiveness of your services and the strength of your relationships with clients.

Another crucial aspect of measuring success lies in financial performance. Detailed financial analysis, including revenue, expenses, and profitability, is imperative for understanding the health of your coaching practice. This data can help in making informed decisions about pricing adjustments, resource allocation, and investment in further business development. Moreover, assessing the return on investment (ROI) for marketing and promotional activities can aid in optimizing your outreach efforts and maximizing the impact of your brand in the coaching industry.

Furthermore, continuing growth in a coaching practice entails staying abreast of industry trends and best practices. Engaging in ongoing professional development, attending relevant workshops, and seeking out mentorship opportunities are essential for honing your skills and knowledge. Networking with other coaches and professionals in related fields can also expand your horizons and provide fresh perspectives. Embracing innovation and technological advancements in coaching tools and methodologies can set you apart and contribute to your sustained success.

Evaluating the scalability of your coaching practice is another vital component of measuring success and ensuring continued growth. As your client base expands and demands evolve, adapting and streamlining your operations becomes paramount. Assessing the efficiency of your processes, leveraging automation where possible, and aligning resources with demand can facilitate scalability while maintaining quality standards. Investing in robust client management systems and agile business solutions can empower you to manage growth effectively and deliver a seamless coaching experience. Finally, maintaining a forward-looking approach is pivotal for continuing growth. Anticipating market shifts and emerging opportunities, diversifying your service offerings, and exploring new client segments are all integral to sustaining momentum. By embracing a mindset of continual improvement and adaptability, you can position your coaching practice for enduring success in a dynamic and competitive landscape.

Ways To Make Extra Income

Online Retail: The Ins and Outs of Selling Clothes

Introduction to Online Retail

Entering the realm of online retail demands a profound understanding of the market dynamics and essential industry-specific considerations. As the digital landscape continues to shape commerce, entrepreneurs venturing into the world of e-commerce must navigate a myriad of factors unique to selling clothing online. This includes recognizing the ever-evolving fashion trends, consumer preferences, and the competitive nature of the apparel market. Moreover, foundational knowledge of online retail principles such as inventory management, website development, and customer engagement strategies are imperative for setting up a successful clothing brand in the virtual sphere. This section aims to delve into the fundamental elements that encompass launching an online clothing store, providing valuable insights on the intricacies of the industry and essential introductory considerations specific to the apparel sector. By gaining a comprehensive grasp of the complexities involved in online retail, aspiring clothing entrepreneurs can adeptly pave their way towards establishing a resilient and thriving presence within the digital marketplace.

Understanding the Apparel Market Landscape

The apparel market landscape is a dynamic and ever-evolving environment that encompasses a wide array of trends, preferences, and consumer behaviors. Understanding this landscape is crucial for any entrepreneur looking to venture into the online retail clothing industry. At its core, the apparel market reflects the collective tastes and demands of consumers, influenced by factors such as fashion trends, cultural shifts, and economic conditions.

One key aspect of comprehending the apparel market landscape is recognizing the diversity within the industry. From fast fashion to sustainable clothing, the market caters to a broad spectrum of consumer preferences and values. Entrepreneurs need to stay abreast of these segments and understand the nuances of each, as it directly impacts product offerings, marketing strategies, and brand positioning.

Moreover, market research plays a pivotal role in understanding the apparel landscape. It involves analyzing consumer behavior, identifying emerging trends, and assessing competitive forces. This data-driven approach provides valuable insights into potential niches, untapped opportunities, and areas for differentiation within the market. By leveraging comprehensive market research, entrepreneurs can make informed decisions and tailor their business strategies to align with market dynamics.

Closely linked to the apparel market landscape is the influence of technology and e-commerce. The digitalization of retail has transformed the way consumers discover, engage with, and purchase clothing items. Online retail platforms, social media, and influencer marketing have redefined the avenues through which fashion products are promoted and sold. Understanding the interplay between technology and the apparel market is essential for navigating the intricacies of online retail and harnessing its potential for business growth.

Furthermore, global and regional trends also shape the apparel market landscape. Whether it's the rise of athleisure wear, the growing demand for sustainable fashion, or the impact of cultural movements on style preferences, being attuned to these trends is critical for staying relevant in the industry. By acknowledging and adapting to these broader shifts, entrepreneurs can align their product offerings with evolving consumer aspirations and market demands.

In essence, understanding the apparel market landscape demands continuous vigilance, adaptability, and a deep appreciation for the multifaceted nature of consumer behavior and industry dynamics. It serves as the foundation upon which successful online retail ventures are built, empowering entrepreneurs to navigate challenges, seize opportunities, and carve a distinctive presence in the bustling world of fashion commerce.

Identifying Your Target Audience

Understanding your target audience is a critical aspect of successful online retail. In the realm of selling clothes, identifying and understanding your potential customers can significantly impact your business's growth and sustainability. The first step in identifying your target audience is to conduct thorough market research. Analyze demographic data such as age, gender, location, income level, and lifestyle preferences to paint a comprehensive picture of your ideal customer. Utilize tools like Google Analytics, social media insights, and industry reports to gather actionable data. Once you have gathered enough information, create buyer personas that represent your different customer segments. These personas should encapsulate the typical characteristics and behaviors of your potential buyers, enabling you to tailor your marketing efforts effectively. Additionally, consider psychographic factors such as values, interests, and purchasing behavior to further refine your understanding of your target audience. Understanding the psychographics of your audience can help inform product choices, branding, and messaging. Communicating with existing and potential customers directly through surveys or interviews also provides valuable insights into their needs, preferences, and pain points. By understanding what motivates your audience's purchasing decisions and what challenges they face, you can tailor your product offerings and marketing strategies accordingly. Furthermore, analyzing the purchasing journey of your target audience can help you identify key touchpoints where your brand can engage with potential customers. For instance, understanding where your audience discovers new products, how they evaluate options, and what prompts them to make a purchase can guide your content strategy and customer engagement tactics. Ultimately, by thoroughly identifying your target audience, you can tailor your product offerings, marketing messages, and overall brand experience to resonate with the specific desires and needs of your potential customers, leading to increased customer satisfaction, loyalty, and sales.

Sourcing Quality Inventory for Your Store

In the realm of online retail, sourcing high-quality inventory is crucial for the success of your clothing store. The items you choose to offer should reflect the tastes and preferences of your target audience while also meeting the standards of excellence that define your brand. To begin this process, it's essential to cultivate relationships with reputable suppliers, whether they are wholesale distributors, manufacturers, or individual designers. Researching potential suppliers will allow you to assess the quality, variety, and pricing of their offerings. In doing so, consider factors such as material quality, design aesthetics, production sustainability, and scalability.

Once you have pinpointed potential suppliers, it's imperative to thoroughly vet them before making any commitments. Requesting samples of their products can provide firsthand insight into the quality and craftsmanship of the items they produce. Beyond product quality, evaluate their reliability, lead times, and customer service. Establishing clear communication and understanding the supplier's policies, such as return procedures and bulk ordering options, will contribute to a seamless and productive partnership.

Furthermore, maintaining diversity in your inventory is key to catering to a range of customer preferences. While curating your selection, strive for a balance of timeless classics, trending pieces, and niche offerings to appeal to various segments of your target demographic. Leveraging tools like trend forecasting reports, customer feedback, and sales data can aid in making informed decisions about which products to include in your inventory.

Seeking out unique, exclusive, or custom-made items can also set your store apart from competitors. Collaborating with independent designers or artisans can present opportunities to feature one-of-a-kind pieces that customers may not find elsewhere, enhancing the distinctive appeal of your brand. Additionally, cultivating an eye for emerging fashion trends and consumer demands will enable you to stay ahead in the ever-evolving world of apparel commerce.

Finally, prioritizing ethical sourcing practices and sustainable materials is increasingly essential for modern consumers. Embracing eco-friendly and socially responsible sourcing methods not only aligns with contemporary values but can also resonate deeply with your customer base. Communicating transparently about your sourcing practices can foster trust and loyalty, forging meaningful connections with conscientious shoppers who value ethical consumption.

In essence, sourcing quality inventory for your online clothing store combines meticulous research, strategic partnerships, and a deep understanding of your customer base. By selecting items that embody both style and substance, you can elevate the shopping experience for your clientele, foster brand loyalty, and position your business for sustained growth and success.

Establishing a Unique Selling Proposition

In the competitive world of online retail, creating a unique selling proposition (USP) is essential for setting your clothing store apart from the countless others vying for consumer attention. Your USP encompasses what makes your brand distinct and sets it apart from competitors. To establish a compelling USP, begin by conducting thorough market research to identify gaps and opportunities in the apparel industry. Understanding consumer needs, preferences, and pain points will provide valuable insights into crafting your USP.

Once you have a clear understanding of your target audience and their expectations, delve into the core values and mission of your brand. What do you stand for, and how does this translate into your products and customer experience? Whether it's sustainable and ethical production practices, unique design aesthetics, or unparalleled customer service, your USP should reflect the essence of your brand.

Moreover, analyzing your competitors' strategies and offerings can guide you in identifying areas where you can differentiate and excel. Differentiation could stem from product quality, innovative designs, customization options, or exceptional after-sales support. Emphasizing the features that set your clothing line apart and provide added value to customers will form the backbone of your USP.

Crafting a memorable brand story that resonates with your target audience is another crucial aspect of establishing a compelling USP. Communicating the narrative behind your brand - be it the inspiration for your designs, your commitment to sustainability, or the journey of your business - adds depth and authenticity to your USP, forging emotional connections with consumers.

Finally, integrating your USP into all facets of your business, from product development to marketing communications, ensures consistency and reinforces your brand identity. This cohesiveness helps build trust and loyalty among your customer base, setting the stage for sustainable success. In summary, your USP serves as the cornerstone of your online clothing store, encapsulating its unique value proposition and fostering meaningful connections with fashion-conscious consumers.

Setting Up an E-commerce Platform

Setting up an e-commerce platform for your clothing line is a crucial step in creating a successful online retail business. The platform serves as the virtual storefront where customers will browse and purchase your products, making it essential to design and optimize the platform for a seamless and engaging user experience. When selecting an e-commerce platform, consider factors such as ease of use, customization options, mobile responsiveness, and integration capabilities with payment gateways and shipping providers. Popular e-commerce platforms like Shopify, WooCommerce, and BigCommerce offer user-friendly interfaces and robust features that cater to the specific needs of clothing retailers. Once you have chosen the right platform, you can begin the process of customizing its appearance and functionality to align with your brand identity and customer preferences.

Customization involves incorporating visually appealing product displays, intuitive navigation menus, and secure checkout processes. High-quality images and detailed product descriptions are essential to convey the unique features of your clothing items and entice customers to make purchases. Additionally, implementing user-friendly filters and search functionalities can help customers find desired products quickly, enhancing their overall shopping experience. It is imperative to prioritize mobile responsiveness, ensuring that your e-commerce platform functions seamlessly across various devices, as a growing number of consumers prefer to shop on their smartphones and tablets.

Furthermore, integrating reliable payment gateways and offering multiple payment options can instill trust and convenience for your customers. This can include credit card payments, digital wallets, and buy now, pay later solutions. Seamless integration with shipping providers is also vital to provide accurate shipping costs and tracking information, which contributes to a positive post-purchase experience. Security is of utmost importance in e-commerce, so ensure that your platform is equipped with robust security measures to safeguard customer data and transactions.

Incorporating features such as customer accounts, wish lists, and personalized recommendations can enhance customer engagement and loyalty. Utilize analytics tools to gain insights into customer behavior, allowing you to refine your marketing strategies and product offerings. Finally, regularly test and optimize your e-commerce platform to address any potential issues and capitalize on emerging trends in online retail. By meticulously setting up and maintaining your e-commerce platform, you can create a compelling online shopping destination for your clothing line, fostering customer satisfaction and driving sales.

Marketing Strategies for Clothing Lines

In the competitive landscape of online retail, effective marketing strategies are essential for the success of clothing lines. When it comes to marketing your apparel products, understanding your target audience is crucial. Utilizing demographic and psychographic data can help tailor your marketing efforts to resonate with potential customers. Leveraging social media platforms such as Instagram, Facebook, and Pinterest allows for visually compelling content to showcase your clothing line and engage with your audience. Utilize high-quality images and compelling storytelling to create an emotional connection with your potential customers. Collaborating with influencers and fashion bloggers can also amplify your brand's visibility and credibility. Additionally, consider implementing email marketing campaigns to nurture relationships with existing customers and attract new ones. Crafting personalized and relevant content in your emails can significantly impact customer retention and conversion rates. Furthermore, optimizing your website for search engines through relevant keywords, meta descriptions, and engaging product descriptions can enhance your online visibility and attract organic traffic. Implementing a robust content marketing strategy through blogs, articles, and fashion tips not only positions your brand as an authority in the industry but also drives traffic to your e-commerce platform. Embracing user-generated content by encouraging customers to share their experiences and photos wearing your clothing can foster a sense of community and authenticity around your brand. Engage with your audience through interactive and informative live sessions, Q&A sessions, and behind-the-scenes glimpses to create a strong bond with your customers. Lastly, leveraging data analytics and performance metrics can provide valuable insights into the effectiveness of your marketing efforts. Monitor key performance indicators such as customer acquisition cost, conversion rates, and customer lifetime value to refine your marketing strategies and allocate resources effectively. By implementing a comprehensive marketing strategy tailored to your clothing line, you can elevate your brand's visibility, connect with your audience on a deeper level, and drive sustainable growth in your online retail business.

Optimizing Customer Experience and Service

To thrive in the competitive landscape of online retail, optimizing customer experience and service is paramount. It involves a comprehensive approach that delves into every touchpoint your customers have with your brand and products. This encompasses a seamless, user-friendly interface on your e-commerce platform, providing detailed product information and high-quality images, and offering various secure payment options. Furthermore, it entails creating an efficient and transparent shipping and return process to instill confidence and trust in your customers.

A crucial element of optimizing customer experience is responsive and personalized customer service. Promptly addressing inquiries and concerns while offering tailored solutions can significantly impact customer satisfaction and loyalty. Implementing live chat support, email assistance, and social media engagement channels allows for effective communication, emphasizing an empathetic and proactive approach to resolving issues.

Additionally, leveraging customer feedback and reviews can provide valuable insights into areas requiring improvement. Actively seeking and implementing constructive criticism fosters continuous enhancement of both products and services. Building a community around your brand through social media involvement and exclusive offers can also cultivate a sense of belonging among your clientele, thus strengthening loyalty and advocacy.

Moreover, placing emphasis on post-purchase engagement is critical. Sending personalized thank-you notes and follow-up emails, as well as offering incentives for future purchases, reinforces positive experiences and promotes customer retention. Every interaction with your brand should leave a lasting impression, fostering an emotional connection and sustaining long-term relationships.

In essence, optimizing customer experience and service goes beyond merely satisfying transactional needs; it aims to create meaningful and memorable interactions that resonate with your audience. By prioritizing excellence in every facet of the customer journey, you position your online retail business for sustained success and growth in a dynamic and evolving market.

Analyzing Sales Data and Metrics

As an online retailer, the ability to analyze sales data and metrics is imperative for making informed decisions that drive business growth and success. Effective analysis of sales data provides valuable insights into customer behavior, product performance, and overall market trends. With the technological advancements in data analytics tools, retailers now have access to a wealth of information that can be leveraged to optimize their strategies and enhance profitability. When delving into sales data analysis, it is essential to start by identifying key performance indicators (KPIs) that align with your business goals. These KPIs may include conversion rates, average order value, customer acquisition cost, and customer lifetime value. By tracking and measuring these metrics, you can gain a comprehensive understanding of your sales performance and identify areas for improvement. Utilizing data visualization techniques such as graphs, charts, and dashboards can further aid in interpreting complex sales data, allowing for easy identification of patterns and trends. Moreover, segmentation of sales data based on various parameters such as demographic information, purchase history, and referral source can provide deeper insights into customer preferences and behaviors. This can be instrumental in tailoring marketing strategies and refining product offerings to better meet consumer needs. Implementing predictive analytics models can also forecast future sales trends and demand patterns, empowering retailers to make proactive decisions and capitalize on emerging opportunities. Furthermore, leveraging data-driven insights can aid in inventory management, ensuring optimal stock levels based on demand fluctuations and seasonal variations. An agile approach to sales data analysis enables retailers to adapt swiftly to market changes and stay ahead of the competition. In conclusion, mastering the art of analyzing sales data and metrics is indispensable for online retail success. It equips retailers with the knowledge and foresight needed to make strategic, data-driven decisions that fuel business growth, enhance customer experiences, and maximize profitability.

Scaling Your Online Retail Business

Scaling your online retail business is a strategic endeavor that requires careful planning and execution. As your business grows, you will need to expand your operations to meet increasing demand while maintaining quality and customer satisfaction. One vital aspect of scaling your online retail business involves optimizing your supply chain and inventory management to accommodate higher sales volumes. This may involve establishing relationships with additional suppliers, improving warehousing and logistics, and implementing efficient inventory tracking systems to minimize stockouts and overstock situations.

Another crucial factor in scaling an online retail business is enhancing the digital infrastructure supporting your e-commerce platform. This includes investing in scalable and robust web hosting services, ensuring website security and stability, and optimizing website performance to handle increased online traffic. As part of this process, consideration should also be given to streamlining the checkout process, integrating convenient payment options, and providing an intuitive and seamless user experience to support higher conversion rates.

In addition to the technical aspects, scaling your online retail business necessitates a focus on marketing and customer acquisition. Leveraging digital advertising, social media outreach, and influencer partnerships can help broaden your brand's reach and attract new customers. It is essential to refine your marketing strategies to effectively communicate your brand's value proposition and unique selling points as you enter new markets or demographics. Moreover, this stage presents an opportunity to cultivate customer loyalty through personalized experiences, loyalty programs, and exceptional customer service, further solidifying your brand's reputation.

Furthermore, scaling an online retail business entails building a strong team and organizational structure to sustain growth. As the demands on your business increase, proper staffing, training, and delegation become imperative. Recruiting individuals with the right skill set and mindset to drive the business forward, while fostering a collaborative and innovative work culture, is paramount. Implementing scalable operational processes, clear communication channels, and leveraging technology for task automation and workflow efficiency are essential in maximizing productivity and maintaining a cohesive and adaptable organization.

Moreover, never overlook the importance of data-driven decision-making when scaling your online retail business. Analyzing key performance indicators, customer behavior, market trends, and competition can provide valuable insights to refine strategies, identify opportunities, and mitigate risks associated with expansion. Data-driven decisions enable informed choices about product assortment, marketing investments, and operational improvements, contributing to sustainable growth and long-term success.

Finally, scaling your online retail business does not solely revolve around expanding internal capabilities; it also involves exploring potential partnerships, collaborations, and distribution channels. Building strategic alliances with complementary brands, seeking distribution agreements with established retailers, or considering international expansion can diversify your revenue streams and introduce your brand to new audiences.

Successfully scaling an online retail business is a multifaceted endeavor that intertwines digital infrastructure enhancement, operational optimization, strategic marketing, organizational development, and informed decision-making. By recognizing the complexities involved and diligently addressing each facet, you can position your online retail business for sustained growth, heightened profitability, and enduring success.

Ways To Make Extra Income

Digital Marketplaces: Navigating Etsy, Shopify, and Beyond

Introduction to Digital Marketplaces

Digital marketplaces play a pivotal role in today's economy, providing a platform for businesses and individuals to showcase and sell their products or services to a global audience. These platforms serve as virtual market hubs, connecting buyers and sellers from diverse backgrounds and locations, fostering a thriving e-commerce ecosystem. The significance of digital marketplaces lies in their ability to level the playing field for small and medium-sized enterprises, empowering them to compete with larger corporations on a global scale. By eliminating the traditional barriers to entry, these marketplaces enable entrepreneurs and artisans to reach a broad customer base without the need for substantial infrastructure or upfront investment. Furthermore, the convenience and accessibility offered by digital marketplaces have transformed consumer behavior, with an increasing number of individuals opting to explore and purchase products online. This shift has reshaped the retail landscape, underscoring the growing influence and relevance of digital marketplaces in shaping modern commerce. As technology continues to advance, digital marketplaces are becoming integral components of both B2C and B2B transactions, serving as dynamic platforms that accommodate a wide range of products and services. Whether it's handcrafted goods, digital downloads, or professional services, these marketplaces provide a versatile and efficient avenue for monetizing offerings. In essence, they foster an environment where innovation thrives, allowing aspiring entrepreneurs and seasoned businesses alike to capitalize on emerging trends and consumer preferences. The interconnected nature of these platforms also contributes to knowledge-sharing and collaboration, promoting a vibrant community of sellers who can learn from each other's experiences and best practices. Through this section, we will delve deeper into the dynamics of digital marketplaces, examining their role in driving economic growth, supporting entrepreneurship, and shaping the future of commerce.

Understanding the Platform Ecosystem

E-commerce has revolutionized the way businesses operate and consumers shop, expanding opportunities through digital marketplaces. Understanding the platform ecosystem is paramount for individuals seeking to capitalize on this evolving landscape. The platform ecosystem refers to the interconnected web of software, applications, and services that facilitate online transactions, connecting buyers and sellers across diverse industries. Central to comprehending this ecosystem is recognizing the variances between different platforms, such as Etsy, Shopify, and other leading marketplaces. This understanding empowers entrepreneurs to make informed decisions about which platform best aligns with their products, target audience, and business objectives. At its core, digital marketplaces provide a virtual space for merchants to showcase and sell their offerings, while offering consumers a convenient and diverse shopping experience.

The intricate nature of the platform ecosystem demands an awareness of the key players, features, and functionality of each marketplace. Factors such as user interface, payment processing, shipping integrations, and customer support vary considerably across platforms. Etsy, for example, caters to creators and artisans, emphasizing handmade, vintage, and unique items, fostering a community ethos. On the contrary, Shopify offers a robust e-commerce infrastructure for businesses of all sizes, providing extensive customization and scalability. Additionally, it's essential for entrepreneurs to consider the support, resources, and tools available within each platform, as these play a pivotal role in optimizing storefront operations and driving sales.

Moreover, integrating with third-party applications and services further enhances the capabilities of digital marketplaces. For instance, plug-ins and extensions enable sellers to leverage marketing tools, analytics, and automation to streamline processes and enhance performance. Understanding the platform ecosystem involves not only mastering the dynamics of individual marketplaces but also grasping the interplay between these platforms and external solutions. By comprehensively understanding the platform ecosystem, entrepreneurs can establish a strong foundation for successful navigation and utilization of digital marketplaces, unlocking opportunities for growth and profitability.

Etsy: Crafting Success in Handmade Markets

Etsy has established itself as a leading digital marketplace for individuals seeking to showcase and sell their handmade and vintage goods. The platform provides artisans, creators, and craftspeople with a dynamic space to exhibit their unique creations to a global audience of discerning buyers and enthusiasts. In the realm of handmade markets, Etsy stands out as an invaluable platform that enables sellers to connect directly with consumers who appreciate artisanal craftsmanship and distinctive products. To find success on Etsy, it is essential to understand the nuances of the platform and employ effective strategies tailored to the preferences and behaviors of its user base. When navigating the Etsy marketplace, sellers must emphasize the story behind their creations. Buyers on Etsy often prioritize the personal touch and narrative woven into each handcrafted item, valuing the connection to the creator and the artistic journey that yields the final product. Hence, crafting a compelling brand narrative and presenting the inspiration and processes behind the handmade pieces can significantly enhance their appeal. Additionally, leveraging high-quality, visually captivating imagery is paramount on Etsy. As a visual-centric platform, striking product photography can serve as a powerful tool for capturing the attention of potential buyers. Furthermore, meticulous attention to detail in product descriptions and titles is crucial for optimizing searchability and enhancing the discoverability of listings. Beyond showcasing individual products, establishing a cohesive brand aesthetic and identity across the storefront reinforces a sense of professionalism and trustworthiness, fostering rapport with customers. Engaging with the vibrant Etsy community through participation in forums, collaborations, and promotional events can amplify visibility and support networking opportunities. Actively involving oneself in the ecosystem not only fosters a sense of camaraderie but also aids in understanding the evolving dynamics and trends within the handmade markets. Lastly, staying abreast of Etsy's policies, fees, and seller guidelines is fundamental for smooth operations and compliance. By immersing themselves in the ethos of Etsy and embracing the values of creativity, authenticity, and community, sellers can forge meaningful connections with patrons and thrive in the realm of handmade markets.

Shopify: Building Your Online Storefront

In today's digital age, establishing an online storefront is essential for entrepreneurs looking to expand their reach and maximize sales potential. Shopify has emerged as one of the leading e-commerce platforms, offering a comprehensive suite of tools and features to help individuals create and manage their online stores with ease. This section delves into the intricacies of utilizing Shopify to build a robust online storefront for your business.

Setting up your Shopify store begins with selecting a visually appealing and intuitive template that aligns with your brand identity and product offerings. Customization options allow you to tailor the storefront to reflect your unique style and showcase your merchandise effectively. Furthermore, Shopify's user-friendly interface empowers users to add products, organize inventory, and implement secure payment gateways seamlessly.

Optimizing your online storefront for search engines is crucial in driving traffic and increasing visibility. With Shopify's built-in SEO tools, you can enhance product descriptions, meta tags, and URLs to improve your store's ranking on search engine results pages. Additionally, leveraging Shopify's integrated analytics enables you to gain valuable insights into customer behavior and preferences, facilitating data-driven decision-making for sales and marketing strategies.

One of the most compelling aspects of Shopify is its flexible and scalable nature. As your business grows, Shopify caters to your evolving needs by providing features such as multi-channel selling, abandoned cart recovery, and customizable discount codes. Seamless integration with social media platforms and third-party apps further extends your store's reach and functionality, fostering a cohesive and effective online selling environment.

Understanding the importance of mobile commerce, Shopify offers responsive themes and mobile-optimized checkout, ensuring a seamless shopping experience for customers across various devices. Moreover, robust security measures and PCI compliance instill trust and confidence in shoppers, thereby reducing cart abandonment and bolstering conversion rates.

Beyond the technical aspects, successful storefront management also involves cultivating a dynamic and engaging customer experience. Utilize Shopify's marketing tools to create targeted campaigns, implement product reviews, and establish loyalty programs that resonate with your audience. By harnessing the power of automation and personalization, you can foster enduring relationships with customers and drive repeat purchases.

In essence, mastering the art of building an online storefront on Shopify empowers entrepreneurs to establish a strong online presence, amplify brand awareness, and capitalize on the boundless opportunities of e-commerce. With a profound understanding of the platform's capabilities and strategic implementation, your Shopify storefront becomes a dynamic engine propelling your business towards sustained growth and prosperity.

Market Analysis and Selection Criteria

As you embark on the journey of navigating digital marketplaces, performing a comprehensive market analysis and honing in on effective selection criteria is pivotal to your success. Market analysis involves evaluating the landscape of your chosen niche within the digital marketplace. Begin by identifying the target audience for your products or services. Understand their needs, preferences, and pain points to tailor your offerings to meet their demands effectively. Leverage data analytics tools to gain insights into consumer behavior and industry trends, thereby informing your business decisions with empirical evidence. Furthermore, examining competitor strategies and marketplace performance can provide valuable benchmarks for your own endeavors.

Selection criteria play a crucial role in determining the optimal digital marketplace for your ventures. Factors such as platform usability, fee structures, and audience demographics should be considered. Assess the compatibility of each platform with the nature of your products or services, ensuring that it aligns with your brand identity and business objectives. Additionally, delve into the level of support and resources offered by the platform to assist sellers in achieving their entrepreneurial goals. Acquiring a deep understanding of the platform's policies, terms of service, and guidelines is equally important to mitigate potential conflicts and navigate the marketplace confidently.

A systematic approach to market analysis and selection criteria empowers entrepreneurs to make informed decisions about where to invest their time and resources within the digital marketplace. By staying attuned to consumer needs and industry dynamics while meticulously evaluating platform suitability, individuals can position themselves strategically to maximize their reach and engagement, ultimately driving growth and success within the competitive landscape of digital commerce. As the technology and e-commerce landscapes continue to evolve, adaptability and agility in response to emerging market trends will be essential for sustaining long-term relevance and profitability in the digital marketplace.

Maximizing Visibility and Reach

To thrive in digital marketplaces such as Etsy, Shopify, and other e-commerce platforms, it is essential to maximize visibility and reach. Achieving this requires a multi-faceted approach that encompasses various strategies and tactics aimed at enhancing brand exposure and connecting with the target audience.

One fundamental strategy for maximizing visibility and reach is through search engine optimization (SEO). By optimizing product titles, descriptions, and tags with relevant keywords, sellers can improve their products' discoverability within the platform's search results. Additionally, utilizing high-quality images and compelling product descriptions can significantly impact click-through rates and capture the attention of potential customers.

In addition to SEO, leveraging social media channels plays a crucial role in expanding reach. Establishing a strong social media presence allows sellers to extend their brand's visibility beyond the confines of the marketplace, reaching a broader audience and driving traffic to their online storefront. Engaging content, strategic use of hashtags, and collaborations with influencers can amplify brand awareness and attract new customers.

Another effective method for expanding reach is by participating in relevant online communities and forums. Joining groups or communities where the target audience congregates enables sellers to interact directly with potential customers, build credibility, and subtly promote their products in a non-intrusive manner. However, it is essential to abide by community guidelines and engage authentically to foster meaningful connections.

Furthermore, capitalizing on email marketing campaigns can be instrumental in reaching both existing and potential customers. Building an email list and sending targeted, personalized messages can nurture relationships with customers, promote new product launches, and drive traffic back to the seller's online store, thereby increasing visibility and sales opportunities.

Moreover, exploring collaborations with other sellers or complementary brands can broaden reach and introduce products to new audiences. Cross-promotional initiatives, joint giveaways, or co-curated collections can leverage each other's customer base and create mutually beneficial opportunities for exposure.

Finally, staying abreast of platform algorithm updates, trends, and changes in consumer behavior is pivotal for adapting visibility strategies. Timely adjustments and continuous experimentation with different approaches will help sellers remain competitive and ensure sustained visibility amidst evolving market dynamics.

Pricing Strategies for Competitive Edge

Pricing strategies play a crucial role in differentiating your offerings and gaining a competitive edge in the digital marketplace landscape. By strategically pricing your products or services, you can effectively communicate value to your target audience while maximizing profitability. The convergence of pricing intelligence and market dynamics can significantly influence consumer behavior and purchasing decisions. Therefore, it's imperative to craft a well-defined pricing strategy that aligns with your overall business goals and resonates with your customer base.

One of the fundamental approaches to pricing involves conducting comprehensive market research to understand the pricing trends and benchmarks within your industry and niche. By analyzing competitors' pricing structures and positioning, you can identify opportunities to price your offerings competitively while emphasizing your unique value proposition. Additionally, leveraging data-driven insights through analytical tools can provide valuable inputs for establishing optimal pricing points, considering factors such as production costs, profit margins, and perceived value.

Another key aspect of pricing strategy is the implementation of dynamic pricing, which involves adjusting prices based on real-time market conditions, demand fluctuations, and competitive activities. This agile approach enables you to capitalize on evolving market dynamics and optimize revenue generation. Through the utilization of algorithms and predictive analytics, businesses can dynamically set prices to reflect varying levels of demand, inventory levels, and seasonal patterns, thereby enhancing competitiveness and responsiveness to market changes.

Furthermore, adopting a value-based pricing model can be instrumental in highlighting the unique benefits and distinctiveness of your products or services. Instead of solely focusing on cost-based pricing, this approach emphasizes the value delivered to customers and their willingness to pay for the outcomes or experiences associated with your offerings. Articulating compelling value propositions and tailoring pricing tiers based on different customer segments can effectively position your brand as a provider of premium solutions, fostering customer loyalty and differentiation in the crowded digital marketplace.

In addition to setting strategic prices, integrating promotional tactics and incentives can bolster customer acquisition and retention efforts. By offering limited-time discounts, bundle deals, or loyalty rewards, businesses can stimulate purchase motivation and cultivate long-term relationships with their customer base. Such promotional strategies not only drive sales but also contribute to building brand equity and sustaining competitive advantages in the digital realm.

Ultimately, a well-crafted pricing strategy should constantly evolve in response to market dynamics and consumer behaviors. Regular evaluation of pricing performance metrics and customer feedback can inform adjustments and refinements, ensuring that your pricing strategies remain aligned with market demands and competitive forces. By prioritizing a strategic approach to pricing, businesses can enhance their market positioning, drive sustainable growth, and thrive in the ever-evolving digital marketplace.

Customer Engagement and Retention

In the competitive landscape of digital marketplaces, customer engagement and retention are vital components for sustainable success. Effective customer engagement goes beyond initial transactions; it fosters long-term relationships, brand loyalty, and advocacy. To achieve this, sellers must prioritize personalized interactions and authentic connections with their customer base. Understanding the needs and preferences of your target audience is fundamental in creating meaningful engagement. Utilizing data analytics and customer feedback can provide valuable insights to tailor products and experiences accordingly. Additionally, leveraging social media platforms and email marketing can further nurture customer relationships, offering exclusive promotions, behind-the-scenes content, and interactive campaigns. Furthermore, establishing a seamless and efficient support system is crucial for addressing concerns and inquiries promptly, thus enhancing the overall customer experience.

Equally significant is the aspect of customer retention. This involves implementing strategies to encourage repeat purchases and minimize churn. Building a strong post-purchase communication strategy through follow-up emails, satisfaction surveys, and personalized recommendations can reinforce the brand-consumer relationship and drive loyalty. Loyalty programs, special perks for returning customers, and membership benefits can also incentivize repeat business. Moreover, creating a robust feedback loop and actively addressing customer issues demonstrates dedication to continuous improvement. Exemplary customer service and consistent product quality are pillars of retaining satisfied customers. Nurturing a community around your brand through user-generated content, forums, and events can further solidify customer loyalty. Additionally, demonstrating corporate social responsibility and ethical practices resonates with modern consumers, contributing to their attachment to the brand. Lastly, adapting to changing consumer behaviors and market trends while maintaining core brand values is essential for long-term success. By fostering authentic connections and offering ongoing value, sellers can proactively engage and retain their customer base, creating a foundation for sustained growth and profitability in digital marketplaces.

Managing Logistics and Fulfillment

To ensure successful operations in digital marketplaces, managing logistics and fulfillment processes is crucial. Efficient logistics management involves overseeing the movement of products from the point of origin to the final destination, while fulfillment encompasses the complete process from receiving an order to delivering the product to the customer's doorstep.

In the realm of eCommerce, establishing a streamlined and reliable logistics network is essential in meeting customer expectations and maintaining a competitive edge in the market. To achieve this, businesses must carefully strategize their inventory management, shipping methods, and order processing systems. Additionally, working closely with trusted carriers or third-party logistics providers can optimize the delivery process and enhance customer satisfaction.

Comprehensive planning and execution are fundamental in ensuring that orders are processed accurately and promptly. This often involves leveraging technology to automate tasks, track shipments in real-time, and communicate transparently with customers regarding their orders. Implementing robust inventory management systems, order tracking software, and efficient warehouse operations play pivotal roles in fulfilling customer demands while minimizing logistical hiccups.

Moreover, the fulfillment stage encompasses the packaging, labeling, and shipping of products. Focusing on environmentally friendly packaging solutions not only aligns with sustainable practices but also emphasizes brand values, contributing to a positive brand image. Leveraging advanced shipping technologies and exploring cost-effective shipping strategies can significantly impact the overall customer experience and contribute to repeat business.

Furthermore, clear communication and proactive engagement with customers throughout the fulfillment process enhance trust and loyalty. This includes providing shipping notifications, resolved inquiries, and accommodating special requests whenever feasible. Creating a seamless and personalized post-purchase experience reinforces brand reputation and fosters long-term customer relationships.

As the eCommerce landscape continues to evolve, embracing innovative logistics solutions and staying abreast of industry trends are imperative. This entails adapting to changes in consumer behavior, advancements in shipping technologies, and developments in supply chain management. By continuously optimizing logistics and fulfillment strategies, businesses can adapt to evolving market dynamics and capitalize on emerging opportunities for growth and expansion.

Future Trends and Strategic Adaptations

As the landscape of digital marketplaces continues to evolve, it is imperative for aspiring entrepreneurs to anticipate and prepare for future trends while staying adaptable and responsive to changes in consumer behavior and technology. Understanding and leveraging these trends can provide a competitive advantage and ensure sustained success in an increasingly dynamic marketplace. One prominent trend is the continued growth of mobile commerce, as more consumers opt for the convenience of shopping via their smartphones and tablets. This necessitates the optimization of digital storefronts for seamless mobile experiences, including responsive designs and user-friendly interfaces. Additionally, the integration of augmented reality (AR) and virtual reality (VR) technologies into online shopping experiences presents exciting opportunities for immersive product interactions and enhanced customer engagement. Entrepreneurs must stay attuned to developments in these areas to remain at the forefront of innovation. Another significant trend to monitor is the increasing demand for sustainable and ethical products. Consumers are placing greater importance on eco-friendly, ethically sourced, and socially responsible goods, prompting a shift towards environmentally conscious offerings. Entrepreneurs should consider aligning their business practices with sustainability initiatives and highlighting these aspects within their marketing efforts. Furthermore, the rise of artificial intelligence (AI) and machine learning algorithms is revolutionizing personalized shopping experiences and predictive analytics. Leveraging AI for targeted product recommendations and hyper-personalized marketing can lead to higher conversion rates and customer satisfaction. It is crucial for digital marketplace sellers to embrace these technologies to deliver tailored experiences that resonate with individual preferences. Adapting to shifting global market dynamics, such as changing trade policies and economic fluctuations, also warrants attention. Entrepreneurs must remain agile in response to geopolitical shifts and economic factors that impact supply chains, shipping costs, and international customer bases. Navigating regulatory changes and trade agreements will be essential for maintaining a competitive edge and mitigating potential disruptions. In conclusion, staying abreast of future trends and strategically adapting to them will be pivotal for thriving in digital marketplaces. By embracing innovations, sustainability, and technological advancements, entrepreneurs can position themselves for long-term viability and relevance in an ever-evolving e-commerce landscape.

Ways To Make Extra Income

Successful Side Hustles

Introduction to Side Hustles: Definitions and Benefits

A side hustle is an endeavor pursued alongside a primary source of income. It represents an opportunity to channel one's skills, passions, and entrepreneurship into a supplementary revenue stream. In today's dynamic and interconnected economy, the concept of side hustles has blossomed, offering individuals the chance to explore their interests while boosting their financial well-being. These ventures often provide a creative outlet for pursuing hobbies or talents that may not be fully utilized in one's day job. The allure of side hustles lies in their capacity to generate additional income, contribute to professional growth, and empower individuals with a sense of autonomy over their financial destiny. The benefits of engaging in a side hustle are manifold. Not only do they offer the potential for increased earnings, but they also provide an avenue for personal development and skill enhancement. Moreover, side hustles allow individuals to diversify their financial portfolio, spreading the risk across multiple income streams and mitigating dependence on a single source of revenue. For many, the pursuit of a side hustle transcends monetary gains; it often signifies a journey of self-discovery, where individuals can transform their passions and hobbies into profitable ventures. As such, side hustles hold the promise of enriching lives, both financially and emotionally, by fostering a deeper connection to one's interests and aspirations. Ultimately, cultivating a successful side hustle demands dedication, resilience, and strategic planning. By delving into this multifaceted approach, individuals can harness the power of side hustles to realize their financial goals, nurture their talents, and chart a more fulfilling career path.

Identifying Marketable Skills and Interests

To succeed in a side hustle, it is essential to identify and leverage your marketable skills and interests. Start by conducting a thorough self-assessment to recognize your areas of expertise, strengths, and passions. Consider both hard skills, such as graphic design, coding, or financial analysis, and soft skills, like communication, problem-solving, and leadership. Reflect on past work experiences, hobbies, and personal projects that have brought you satisfaction or recognition. These can often reveal valuable indications of where your true talents lie.

Once you have identified your core competencies, seek feedback from mentors, colleagues, and even friends and family members who can offer an external perspective on your abilities. Their insights can shed light on skills you may not have recognized in yourself and provide valuable guidance on how to best utilize them within a side hustle.

In addition to skills, consider your personal interests and passions. What activities or topics do you find captivating? What subjects do you enjoy learning about or discussing in your leisure time? These interests can serve as fertile ground for potential side hustle ideas. For example, if you are passionate about fitness, you might explore opportunities in personal training, wellness coaching, or developing health-related products.

Furthermore, examine industry trends and market demands to align your skills and interests with lucrative opportunities. Stay informed about emerging markets, consumer preferences, and technological advancements that could create avenues for your expertise. Research online platforms, social media discussions, and industry publications to gain insights into which niches are currently thriving and which are projected to grow in the future.

Remember that the ideal side hustle combines both profitability and personal fulfillment. Therefore, ensure that your chosen venture not only capitalizes on your skills but also resonates with your genuine interests. By identifying marketable skills and interests that intersect with current opportunities, you set a strong foundation for a successful and rewarding side hustle.

Researching Potential Opportunities and Niches

When delving into the realm of side hustles, it is essential to thoroughly research potential opportunities and niches to identify a market gap or an area with high demand. This extensive research phase serves as the foundation for your side hustle's success and longevity. Start by immersing yourself in industry-specific publications, online forums, and social media groups to gain insight into emerging trends and consumer needs. Conduct market analysis to understand the competitive landscape, target audience preferences, and pricing strategies adopted by existing players. It's crucial to evaluate not only the current market condition but also its future potential, considering factors such as technological advancements, demographic shifts, and economic forecasts. By identifying gaps in the market or areas with untapped potential, you can position your side hustle for maximum impact and sustainable growth. Additionally, consider conducting surveys or reaching out to your network to gather firsthand feedback on potential products or services. This qualitative data can provide valuable insights into customer pain points, desires, and unmet needs. Moreover, explore different demographics and psychographics to tailor your offerings effectively. For instance, if you're considering a freelance graphic design business, research various industries and their specific design requirements to target niche markets such as tech startups, wellness brands, or e-commerce ventures. Diversification of potential opportunities and niches can also involve exploring multiple channels or platforms through which to offer your goods or services. Whether it's through e-commerce platforms, local markets, or digital freelance marketplaces, thorough research will help you identify the most promising channels and assess the associated risks and benefits. Ultimately, the depth of your research and understanding of potential opportunities and niches will significantly influence the traction and profitability of your side hustle. By strategically identifying and analyzing these focal points, you can better position yourself in the market and increase the likelihood of establishing a successful and sustainable side venture.

Time Management Strategies for Balancing Main Job and Side Hustle

Balancing a full-time job with a side hustle requires meticulous time management and prioritization. Effective time management is crucial to avoid burnout and ensure optimal productivity in both professional and entrepreneurial pursuits. To achieve this balance, individuals must first assess their current commitments and develop a clear understanding of the time available for their side hustle. Creating a detailed schedule outlining work hours, personal responsibilities, and dedicated time for the side hustle can serve as a foundational tool for effective time management.

Incorporating time-blocking techniques can be highly beneficial in managing various tasks associated with the main job and the side hustle. By allocating specific time slots for different activities, individuals can maintain focus and reduce the likelihood of feeling overwhelmed by conflicting priorities. It is important to identify peak productivity hours and leverage them for the most demanding tasks, whether it be your main job or side hustle. Moreover, utilizing productivity tools and apps can streamline task management and enhance overall efficiency.

Effective delegation and outsourcing can also play a significant role in time management. For individuals juggling a full-time job and a side hustle, delegating non-essential tasks at work and seeking assistance with certain aspects of the side hustle can alleviate time constraints and reduce stress. This could involve hiring freelancers for specific projects or collaborating with partners who can share the workload effectively. Delegation not only frees up time but also allows individuals to focus on high-priority tasks that directly contribute to their professional and entrepreneurial growth.

Maintaining a proper work-life balance is indispensable when pursuing multiple endeavors. Scheduling regular breaks, engaging in physical activity, and prioritizing self-care are essential elements of effective time management, promoting overall well-being and sustainable productivity. Additionally, open communication with employers and colleagues about the side hustle can foster understanding and support, potentially leading to flexible arrangements that accommodate both professional and entrepreneurial activities.

Lastly, adapting a proactive mindset and being adaptable to change is fundamental in managing time effectively as a side hustler. Embracing unexpected challenges with resilience, continuously reassessing time management strategies, and adapting to evolving priorities will empower individuals to navigate the complexities of balancing a main job and a burgeoning entrepreneurial venture. By implementing these strategies, individuals can cultivate a harmonious synergy between their professional career and their side hustle, maximizing productivity, and achieving long-term success.

Developing a Business Plan for Your Side Hustle

A well-crafted business plan is vital for the success of your side hustle. It serves as a roadmap, guiding your efforts and providing clarity on your objectives, target market, and financial projections. The first step in developing a business plan is to clearly define your business idea and goals. What problem does your side hustle solve? Who is your target audience, and how will you reach them? Conduct thorough market research to understand your industry, competitors, and potential customers. Analyze the demand for your product or service and identify any gaps in the market that your side hustle can fill. Additionally, outline the unique value proposition that sets your side hustle apart from others. With this foundational knowledge, you can develop a solid business model for your side hustle. This includes determining your revenue streams, pricing strategy, and sales channels. Create a detailed marketing plan that outlines how you will promote and sell your offerings. Consider the most effective marketing tools and tactics for reaching your target audience, such as social media, content marketing, or partnerships with complementary businesses. Your business plan should also include a comprehensive financial forecast. Estimate your startup costs, ongoing expenses, and projected revenue. Develop a realistic budget and identify potential sources of funding if needed. Furthermore, establish key performance indicators (KPIs) to track the progress and success of your side hustle. Set measurable goals and milestones, allowing you to assess your performance and make informed strategic decisions. Lastly, revisit and revise your business plan regularly. As your side hustle evolves and market conditions change, your business plan should adapt accordingly. Continuously monitor your financials, adjust your marketing strategies, and refine your goals to ensure the long-term sustainability and growth of your side hustle.

Marketing Tactics to Promote Your Side Hustle

When it comes to promoting your side hustle, effective marketing tactics play a crucial role in reaching and engaging potential customers. Without proper promotion, even the most innovative side hustle may struggle to gain traction in the market. This section will delve into a variety of strategic marketing techniques that can elevate the visibility and profitability of your endeavor.

First and foremost, understanding your target audience is paramount. Research and analyze the demographics, preferences, and behaviors of your potential customers to tailor your marketing efforts effectively. Whether through social media insights, online surveys, or direct interactions, gaining insights into your audience will guide your promotional strategies.

In the digital age, leveraging social media platforms is an indispensable avenue for promoting your side hustle. Crafting compelling and visually captivating content on platforms like Instagram, Facebook, and LinkedIn can significantly expand your reach. Engage with your audience through regular posts, stories, and interactive features, fostering a sense of community around your side hustle.

Furthermore, consider the power of influencer collaborations. Partnering with relevant influencers in your niche can expose your side hustle to a wider audience and build credibility. Vet potential collaborators carefully to ensure alignment with your brand ethos and target demographic.

Email marketing remains a stalwart tactic for nurturing leads and driving conversions. Building an email list enables you to communicate directly with interested individuals, providing exclusive updates, promotions, and personalized offerings. Implementing automated email campaigns can streamline this process, enhancing efficiency while maintaining a personal touch.

Another impactful strategy involves search engine optimization (SEO). By optimizing your website and content to rank higher in search engine results, you can attract organic traffic and amplify your visibility. Conduct keyword research and create valuable, keyword-rich content that resonates with your audience while adhering to best SEO practices.

Additionally, don't overlook the potential of partnerships and collaborations with complementary businesses or influencers. Mutual promotion and cross-marketing endeavors can introduce your side hustle to new audiences and establish valuable connections within your industry.

Lastly, measuring the efficacy of your marketing efforts is essential. Utilize analytical tools and performance metrics to assess the impact of your campaigns, identifying successful strategies and areas for improvement. This data-driven approach empowers you to refine your marketing tactics continually, optimizing your promotional endeavors for sustained growth.

By integrating a blend of these marketing tactics tailored to your specific side hustle, you can cultivate a robust promotional strategy that maximizes your outreach, fosters customer engagement, and propels the success of your entrepreneurial pursuit.

Leveraging Technology and Tools for Efficiency

In today's fast-paced digital landscape, technology plays a pivotal role in enhancing the efficiency and productivity of side hustles. Leveraging the right tools can streamline various aspects of your business, from operations and customer interaction to marketing and financial management. One of the key areas where technology can significantly impact side hustles is in automating repetitive tasks. By utilizing tools such as project management software, email marketing platforms, and social media schedulers, entrepreneurs can free up valuable time that can be redirected towards strategic decision-making and business growth. Additionally, embracing cloud-based solutions and digital storage not only ensures seamless access to critical data but also facilitates collaboration with remote team members or freelancers. Furthermore, harnessing analytics tools enables entrepreneurs to gain valuable insights into customer behavior, market trends, and the performance of their products or services. This data-driven approach empowers them to make informed decisions, optimize their offerings, and tailor their marketing strategies for maximum impact. Moreover, adopting e-commerce platforms and website builders provides aspiring entrepreneurs with the means to establish a professional online presence and reach a wider audience. This accessibility can be further amplified by integrating secure payment gateways and optimizing the user experience. It is essential for entrepreneurs to stay abreast of emerging technologies and trends within their industry. Regularly updating and adapting their toolset allows them to remain competitive and agile in the ever-evolving market. Additionally, leveraging the power of social media and digital advertising platforms can amplify the reach and impact of promotional efforts. Implementing targeted campaigns and monitoring their performance through analytics can help in refining marketing strategies for optimal results. As technology continues to advance, the potential for innovation and efficiency within side hustles grows exponentially. Entrepreneurs who embrace these advancements and integrate them thoughtfully into their operations are better positioned to scale their businesses, serve their customers effectively, and achieve sustainable success.

Case Studies of Successful Side Hustles

The best way to gain insight and inspiration for your own side hustle is by studying real-life success stories. In this section, we will delve into a series of case studies showcasing individuals who have effectively turned their side hustles into thriving businesses. Each case study will provide a detailed account of the entrepreneur's journey, including the initial idea, challenges faced, strategies employed, and the eventual triumph. From freelance content creators to e-commerce entrepreneurs, these case studies will highlight the diverse range of opportunities available and offer valuable lessons on what it takes to succeed in the world of side hustles. By examining these real-world examples, you will gain practical knowledge and actionable takeaways that can be applied to your own entrepreneurial endeavors. These case studies will serve as an invaluable source of motivation, illustrating how determination, innovation, and strategic thinking can lead to the transformation of a simple side gig into a profitable and sustainable venture. Additionally, the diversity of industries and business models presented in these case studies will demonstrate that success in the realm of side hustles is not limited to any specific field or skill set. Regardless of your background or expertise, the experiences shared in these case studies will offer valuable insights and strategies that are universally applicable. Moreover, by analyzing both the successes and obstacles encountered by these entrepreneurs, you will gain a comprehensive understanding of the realistic challenges and rewards associated with building and growing a side hustle. This knowledge will empower you to make informed decisions, anticipate potential hurdles, and proactively develop effective solutions for your own entrepreneurial journey. Ultimately, through the exploration of these compelling case studies, you will be equipped with the wisdom and inspiration needed to embark on your own path towards transforming a passionate hobby or skill into a lucrative and fulfilling side hustle.

Common Challenges and How to Overcome Them

One of the most common challenges faced by individuals pursuing a side hustle is the difficulty in managing precious time. Balancing a full-time job with a side gig can be overwhelming, leading to fatigue and potential burnout. To overcome this challenge, it's essential to prioritize tasks effectively, delegate responsibilities if possible, and establish a clear schedule. Additionally, leveraging technology and automation tools can streamline processes and free up valuable time. Another prevalent difficulty revolves around the uncertainty of generating consistent income from a side hustle. Many aspiring entrepreneurs may encounter fluctuations in earnings, causing financial stress. To address this concern, diversifying income streams within the side hustle, and implementing strategic financial planning can provide stability during lean periods. Moreover, networking and seeking mentorship from experienced individuals in your chosen industry can offer valuable insights and guidance on overcoming financial hurdles. Furthermore, overcoming self-doubt and imposter syndrome is an obstacle that many side hustlers face. The fear of failure or comparison to others' success can hinder progress. It's crucial to cultivate resilience and self-confidence through continuous learning, seeking feedback, and celebrating small victories. Surrounding oneself with a supportive community and seeking inspiration from successful entrepreneurs can also combat feelings of self-doubt. Additionally, navigating legal and regulatory requirements can pose significant obstacles for side hustlers. Understanding the necessary permits, tax implications, and compliance standards is vital to avoid legal setbacks. Seeking professional advice and using reliable resources, such as government websites or legal forums, can provide clarity on complex legal matters. Lastly, maintaining a healthy work-life balance while juggling a full-time job and a side hustle remains a persistent challenge. Setting clear boundaries and establishing designated 'off' times for both work commitments can help prevent burnout and foster overall well-being. Incorporating regular physical activity, mindfulness practices, and spending quality time with loved ones is imperative for maintaining equilibrium. Embracing these strategies can help navigate common challenges encountered during the pursuit of a successful side hustle.

Evaluating Growth and Transitioning to Full-Time

Evaluating the growth of your side hustle is a critical step in determining whether it has the potential to become a full-time occupation. As your side business expands, you must assess various factors to make an informed decision about transitioning to full-time entrepreneurship. One key aspect to consider is financial stability. Analyze your side hustle's revenue trajectory, profitability, and sustainability over time. Evaluate whether it can consistently cover your living expenses and provide a comparable income to your current job. Assess the scalability of your venture and identify opportunities for further growth. Understanding the market demand and potential for expansion is essential when considering the transition to full-time. Additionally, consider the personal impact of pursuing your side hustle as a primary occupation. Reflect on your passion and motivation for the venture, ensuring that the transition aligns with your long-term goals and aspirations. Acknowledge the potential challenges and sacrifices involved in becoming a full-time entrepreneur, and prepare yourself for the necessary commitment and dedication required. It is crucial to evaluate the lifestyle changes and potential risks associated with transitioning to a full-time pursuit. Seek feedback from mentors, industry professionals, and trusted advisors to gain valuable insights and perspectives on your decision. Create a detailed transition plan outlining the steps and milestones for moving from a part-time endeavor to a full-time career. Define clear objectives and measurable goals to guide your transition process. Prepare financially by establishing an emergency fund and minimizing personal debt to mitigate the financial uncertainties of entrepreneurship. Develop a comprehensive marketing and sales strategy to expand your customer base and reach new markets as you transition to full-time operation. Finally, consider the legal and administrative aspects of formalizing your business structure and complying with regulatory requirements as a full-time entrepreneur. Whether it involves registering your company, obtaining necessary licenses, or seeking professional guidance, ensure that you are well-prepared for the legal and operational aspects of running your business full-time. By thoroughly evaluating the growth of your side hustle and strategically planning the transition to full-time entrepreneurship, you can embark on this journey with confidence and determination.

Ways To Make Extra Income

Building Passive Income Streams

Introduction to Passive Income

Passive income, an increasingly discussed topic in the financial world, stands as a powerful concept that contrasts with traditional 'active' income. It revolves around the principle of earning money with minimal ongoing effort, often through investments in assets or businesses that can generate revenue without constant direct involvement. This approach aims to break free from the limitations of trading time for money and instead focuses on leveraging initial investments of time, capital, or both, to establish continuous streams of income.

As the concept continues to gain traction, individuals are becoming more interested in diversifying their income sources beyond conventional employment. This shift is driven by the appeal of supplementing—or even replacing—active income with money-making opportunities that require less day-to-day attention and allow for greater flexibility and independence. Understanding the fundamentals of passive income is crucial for anyone looking to embark on this journey toward financial freedom and security.

One of the key principles underlying passive revenue generation is the recognition that building sustainable income streams often requires an upfront investment. This might take the form of allocating resources into income-generating assets, such as real estate properties, dividend-yielding stocks, or creating digital products. The goal is to plant the seeds of future income by committing resources today in a way that will yield returns over the long term.

Furthermore, passive income strategies also emphasize the importance of scalability and leverage, aiming to maximize the potential for generating earnings with minimal additional effort. By strategically deploying resources and optimizing processes, individuals can create systems that continue to produce income with reduced active participation, allowing for the potential of wealth accumulation and financial stability.

The realm of passive income is vast and diverse, encompassing various vehicles and approaches suited to different risk appetites, interests, and capacities. Investors may explore real estate investments, dividend stocks, online businesses, intellectual property, automated business models, and more, each offering unique avenues for building passive income streams.

In essence, the pursuit of passive income involves a paradigm shift from solely relying on earned income to cultivating sustainable, self-perpetuating revenue sources. By delving into this domain, individuals open themselves up to the potential of financial abundance and freedom, shaping a pathway towards a more secure and prosperous future.

Understanding the Principles of Passive Revenue Generation

Passive income is the holy grail of financial success, offering the promise of ongoing earnings with limited ongoing effort. It is essential to develop a deep understanding of the principles that underpin this revenue generation strategy. The concept of passive income revolves around building systems and investments that generate wealth with minimal direct involvement. This form of income is often derived from assets such as real estate properties, stocks, bonds, or intellectual property, among other sources. Understanding the fundamental principles of passive revenue generation requires a comprehensive look at the mechanisms through which these earnings are generated. It involves recognizing the difference between active and passive income, understanding the time and resources required to establish passive streams, and identifying the various sources from which passive income can be derived. Moreover, developing a keen awareness of the factors that influence the sustainability and growth of passive income streams is crucial. This entails delving into concepts such as compounding returns, leverage, and market dynamics. Additionally, it is indispensable to grasp the role of risk management in maintaining passive income sources. This involves assessing and mitigating potential risks associated with various investment vehicles and income-generating activities. To truly comprehend the principles of passive revenue generation, one must also explore the psychological and behavioral aspects linked to long-term wealth creation. Understanding the motivations, mindset, and discipline required to sustain passive income streams over time is paramount. Furthermore, an examination of macroeconomic factors, industry trends, and technological advancements that impact passive income sources provides valuable insights. Mastering the principles of passive income lays the foundation for aspiring individuals to establish a secure and sustainable financial future. This knowledge empowers them to make informed decisions, implement effective strategies, and adapt to evolving economic landscapes. Armed with a thorough comprehension of these principles, individuals can optimize their efforts to build enduring passive income streams and achieve financial freedom.

Investment Strategies for Long-Term Gains

As individuals seek to establish and grow their passive income streams, considering various investment strategies for long-term gains becomes paramount. Investing with a long-term perspective involves aligning one's financial goals with well-thought-out and disciplined approaches that prioritize sustained profitability and stability. When formulating an investment strategy geared towards long-term gains, it is crucial to consider several key factors. Diversification of the investment portfolio emerges as a fundamental principle, enabling investors to spread their assets across different asset classes, thus reducing overall risk. By diversifying across varying sectors and industries, investors can mitigate the impact of market volatility and potential downturns. Another vital aspect involves conducting thorough research and analysis before making any investment decisions, considering both macroeconomic trends and the specific performance of individual securities. This approach allows investors to spot opportunities and anticipate potential risks, contributing to informed decision-making. Furthermore, maintaining a long-term outlook entails a commitment to weather short-term fluctuations in asset values, focusing on the underlying fundamentals of the investments rather than reacting impulsively to market movements. A buy-and-hold strategy is often advocated in this context, emphasizing the retention of investments over extended periods to capitalize on the power of compounding returns. Strategic asset allocation also plays a critical role in long-term investment success, balancing risk and reward by apportioning investments across various asset classes according to one's risk tolerance and financial objectives. Additionally, integrating tax-efficient investment strategies can significantly enhance the long-term growth and preservation of wealth. By employing tax-advantaged accounts and maximizing the benefits of tax-deferred investment vehicles, individuals can optimize their overall returns while minimizing tax liabilities. As the global economic landscape evolves, embracing sustainable and socially responsible investment practices has gained prominence. Ethical, environmental, and governance considerations are increasingly factored into long-term investment strategies, aligning financial objectives with the broader values and responsibilities of investors. Finally, particularly for those venturing into passive real estate investments, strategic property selection and management play pivotal roles in securing enduring income streams. Whether through commercial or residential properties, careful evaluation of location, rental potential, and property management efficiencies is imperative for long-term gains. Implementing these investment strategies for long-term gains requires a diligent and forward-thinking approach, empowering individuals to position themselves for sustained financial prosperity and security.

Real Estate: Creating Residual Income Opportunities

Real estate investment is a fundamental pillar of creating passive income streams. The inherent value and potential for appreciation make it an attractive avenue for generating long-term wealth. When considering real estate as a means to create residual income, the focus shifts from the traditional buy-and-sell approach to leveraging properties for rental income or property appreciation. One of the key strategies in real estate investment for generating passive income is the acquisition of rental properties. This involves purchasing residential or commercial properties and leasing them to tenants. Through this method, investors can benefit from regular rental payments, which contribute to a consistent stream of passive income. Additionally, real estate also offers the potential for passive income through property appreciation. As the demand for properties increases over time, the value of real estate assets appreciates, allowing investors to realize substantial gains without actively participating in day-to-day operations. Another avenue within real estate investment for generating residual income is through real estate crowdfunding platforms. These platforms enable investors to pool their resources with others to invest in larger real estate projects, such as commercial developments or multi-unit residential properties. By diversifying across various projects, investors can benefit from passive income generated by rental income or property appreciation. Real estate investment trusts (REITs) are another popular option for individuals seeking passive income through real estate. REITs are companies that own, operate, or finance income-generating real estate across a range of property sectors. Investing in REITs allows individuals to access the benefits of real estate ownership without the need for direct property management. Furthermore, passive income from real estate investments often yields tax advantages, including deductions for mortgage interest, property depreciation, and operating expenses. It is important to note that while real estate presents lucrative opportunities for residual income, it also requires careful evaluation of market conditions, property management, and risk mitigation strategies. Successful real estate investors prioritize due diligence, engage in comprehensive market research, and employ effective management practices to maximize the potential for passive income generation. Embracing real estate as a means to create residual income opportunities demands a strategic approach and ongoing commitment to optimizing property performance and capitalizing on market trends.

Dividend Stocks: Building Wealth Through the Market

Investing in dividend stocks provides an effective means of generating passive income and building long-term wealth. Dividend stocks are shares of companies that distribute a portion of their earnings to shareholders on a regular basis, often quarterly. This consistent income stream can be a valuable addition to an individual's investment portfolio. When selecting dividend stocks, it is crucial to consider various factors including the company's track record of paying dividends, its financial stability, and the sustainability of the dividend payments. Additionally, investors should assess the yield, which is the percentage of the stock's price that the dividends represent. A higher yield may indicate a higher income potential, but it is essential to evaluate this in conjunction with other metrics to ensure the stock is a sound investment. Diversifying across different sectors and industries can also help mitigate risk and enhance the overall stability of the investment portfolio. Moreover, reinvesting dividends through a dividend reinvestment plan (DRIP) can compound returns over time, accelerating the growth of the investment. It is important to conduct thorough research and due diligence before making any investment decisions, as the stock market can be influenced by various external factors and fluctuate unpredictably. Finally, monitoring and reviewing the performance of dividend stocks regularly allows for informed decision-making and adjustments to the investment strategy. By strategically selecting dividend stocks and adopting a long-term perspective, investors can leverage the power of compounding returns to build substantial wealth and create a reliable source of passive income.

Online Ventures: Monetizing Digital Platforms

In today's interconnected world, there are abundant opportunities for creating passive income through online ventures. Monetizing digital platforms offers a wide array of possibilities for individuals seeking to diversify their income streams and build long-term wealth. One of the most prevalent methods of generating passive income online is through affiliate marketing. By promoting products or services on websites, blogs, and social media channels, individuals can earn commissions on sales referred through their unique affiliate links. This strategy not only allows for flexibility in terms of content creation but also offers the potential for exponential growth as the audience expands. Additionally, creating and selling digital products can be a lucrative endeavor. E-books, online courses, stock photos, and software are just a few examples of digital products that can generate passive income over an extended period. Developing valuable content that resonates with a target audience is essential for establishing a sustainable source of passive revenue. Furthermore, leveraging the power of e-commerce platforms can provide substantial passive income opportunities. Establishing an online store and utilizing dropshipping or print-on-demand services enable individuals to sell physical products without the need for inventory management or order fulfillment. With the right marketing and product selection, this approach can yield significant passive income. Another avenue for monetizing digital platforms involves creating and monetizing a YouTube channel or podcast. With engaging content and a loyal following, creators can earn advertising revenue, sponsorships, and donations, turning their passion into a consistent source of passive income. Moreover, developing mobile apps or online tools that cater to specific needs or interests can result in recurring revenue from subscriptions, in-app purchases, or advertising. Building a user base and providing continual value are key factors in maximizing passive income potential in this domain. It's crucial to recognize that while online ventures offer promising opportunities for passive income, success often requires dedication, strategic planning, and ongoing optimization. As the digital landscape continues to evolve, staying informed about emerging trends and adapting to changes is essential for sustaining and growing passive income from online endeavors.

Leveraging Intellectual Property for Continuous Earnings

Intellectual property (IP) represents a crucial asset in the quest for sustainable income streams. Whether in the form of patents, trademarks, copyrights, or trade secrets, IP holds the potential to generate continuous earnings through its utilization and strategic exploitation. In an era dominated by digital advancements, the significance of IP in revenue generation has only amplified. This chapter delves into the multifaceted realm of leveraging intellectual property for continuous earnings and examines various avenues through which individuals and businesses can capitalize on their IP assets. The concept of licensing stands as an eminent strategy in monetizing IP. By granting permission to others for the use of their IP, creators and owners can lucratively earn royalties while retaining ownership rights. Furthermore, establishing brand value through trademarks can fortify the market presence and enable higher pricing power, thus driving enhanced revenues and earning potential. Additionally, the competitive advantage conferred by protected IP can provide a significant edge in negotiations and collaborations, leading to improved financial outcomes. An in-depth exploration of IP commercialization avenues such as franchising, joint ventures, and strategic partnerships unveils the myriad opportunities for ensuring continuous earnings from intellectual property. It is imperative to also consider the legal nuances and protective measures surrounding the exploitation of IP, safeguarding against infringement and unauthorized usage. The proactive pursuit of IP protection through registration and vigilant monitoring enables a robust defence of these valuable assets, thereby consolidating the prospects for sustainable earnings. Moreover, leveraging IP for continuous earnings necessitates a comprehensive understanding of market trends, consumer behavior, and evolving industry landscapes. By aligning the monetization of IP with market demands and technological advancements, individuals and organizations can maximize the revenue potential and cultivate enduring streams of income. Collaboration with legal and financial experts in the domain of IP management and monetization can further enhance the efficacy of leveraging intellectual property for continuous earnings, reinforcing the legitimacy and profitability of these pursuits. As the economic landscape continues to evolve, the adept navigation of IP-based revenue models holds substantial promise for individuals and enterprises aspiring to cultivate resilient, continuous income streams. Leveraging intellectual property strategically and ethically not only offers a pathway to sustained earnings but also fosters innovation, creativity, and enterprise in the ever-evolving global marketplace.

Automated Business Models: Efficiency and Prosperity

As the modern business landscape continues to evolve, automated business models have emerged as a powerful means of achieving efficiency, scalability, and sustained prosperity. These innovative models leverage technology and streamlined processes to minimize manual intervention while maximizing output and profitability. They encompass a diverse range of industries and applications, from e-commerce platforms that utilize automated inventory management and fulfillment systems to digital marketing strategies that harness AI algorithms for targeted customer engagement.

One of the key advantages of automated business models is their ability to streamline repetitive tasks, freeing up human resources to focus on higher-value activities such as strategic planning, innovation, and customer relationship management. By implementing automated workflows and systems, organizations can reduce operational overheads, increase productivity, and enhance overall agility in responding to market dynamics. This efficiency not only drives cost savings but also fosters a culture of continuous improvement and adaptability.

Moreover, automated business models play a pivotal role in unlocking new revenue streams and expanding market reach. Through predictive analytics and machine learning algorithms, businesses can harness data-driven insights to optimize pricing strategies, forecast demand patterns, and personalize offerings, thereby increasing sales and customer retention. Additionally, automation enables seamless integration across various functions, fostering cross-channel coherence and delivering cohesive customer experiences—a cornerstone of sustainable growth in today's competitive marketplace.

Furthermore, the adoption of automated business models empowers entrepreneurs and enterprises to achieve scalability without linear increases in resource allocation. By automating core processes, businesses can efficiently handle surges in workload, expand into new markets, and seamlessly onboard new customers without incurring prohibitive incremental costs or compromising service quality. The resulting ability to scale quickly and efficiently positions organizations for long-term success and resilience amidst fluctuating market conditions and evolving consumer demands.

Nevertheless, it is imperative for businesses to prudently navigate the complexities and potential pitfalls associated with automated business models. While automation offers manifold benefits, it also introduces dependencies on technology infrastructure, data security considerations, and the need for stringent quality assurance measures to uphold reliability and trust. Furthermore, the ethical implications of automated decision-making and the impact on the workforce necessitate thoughtful evaluation and proactive mitigation strategies to ensure responsible and sustainable implementation.

In conclusion, automated business models represent a transformative paradigm in contemporary commerce, driving operational excellence, stimulating innovation, and catalyzing sustainable growth. Leveraging the synergies of technology, data, and human ingenuity, these models are poised to redefine the possibilities of efficiency, productivity, and prosperity for businesses across diverse sectors and scales of operation.

Managing Risks in Passive Investments

Passive investments are often considered a reliable means of generating long-term income without active involvement. However, as with any form of investment, they carry inherent risks that must be thoroughly assessed and managed. Understanding and effectively managing these risks is pivotal to the sustainability and success of passive income streams.

One key risk associated with passive investments is market volatility. Market fluctuations can significantly impact the value of assets such as stocks, bonds, and real estate, potentially leading to financial losses. Diversification across various asset classes and continuous monitoring of market trends are essential strategies for mitigating this risk. Additionally, staying informed about economic indicators, geopolitical events, and industry-specific factors can help investors anticipate and respond to market volatility.

Another critical risk to consider is inflation. Over time, inflation erodes the purchasing power of money, affecting the returns on investment. Passive income streams must therefore outpace inflation to ensure sustained wealth accumulation. Assets that have historically shown resilience against inflation, such as real estate and dividend-paying stocks, can serve as effective hedges against this risk.

Moreover, interest rate risk poses a significant threat to certain passive investments. For instance, fixed-income securities like bonds are vulnerable to fluctuations in interest rates, which can impact their market value. Understanding the inverse relationship between bond prices and interest rates is imperative for investors seeking to minimize the impact of interest rate risk on their portfolios.

Legal and regulatory risks also warrant careful consideration when engaging in passive investments. Changes in tax laws, government regulations, or compliance requirements can influence the profitability and viability of investment avenues. Seeking professional guidance and staying abreast of legal developments can assist in navigating this complex landscape and ensuring adherence to regulatory standards.

Furthermore, liquidity risk pertains to the ease of converting an investment into cash without significant loss of value. Some passive investments may lack liquidity, meaning that selling them quickly at fair market value could be challenging. Evaluating the liquidity characteristics of potential investments is crucial, particularly in times of financial uncertainty or unexpected cash needs.

Additionally, credit risk is a vital concern when investing in fixed-income securities or debt instruments. It refers to the possibility of a borrower failing to fulfill their financial obligations, thereby affecting the return on investment. Thorough credit analysis and diversification in credit exposures are fundamental measures for managing credit risk in passive investment portfolios.

Overall, diligent risk management practices are indispensable for individuals seeking to build and safeguard passive income streams. By proactively identifying, assessing, and implementing strategies to mitigate these risks, investors can enhance the resilience and profitability of their investment portfolios.

Concluding Insights and Path Forward

In wrapping up our discussion on passive income generation, it is imperative to take a moment to reflect on the key insights gained and chart a course for future endeavors. Building passive income streams is not just about financial gain; it is a mindset shift towards creating sustainable wealth and achieving long-term financial freedom. The journey we have undertaken has been filled with valuable lessons and practical strategies that can serve as the foundation for individuals seeking to diversify their income sources. As we look forward, it is essential to maintain a forward-thinking approach and adapt to the evolving landscape of passive revenue generation. Embracing innovation and staying informed about emerging opportunities will be fundamental in this pursuit.

One of the critical insights gleaned from our exploration is the significance of understanding and mitigating risks associated with passive investments. It's crucial to conduct thorough due diligence and carefully evaluate potential opportunities for long-term viability and stability. By proactively managing risks, investors can position themselves to capitalize on lucrative passive income streams while safeguarding their financial well-being. Additionally, fostering a diversified portfolio is instrumental in spreading risk and optimizing returns. This balanced approach ensures resilience and minimizes exposure to unforeseen market fluctuations and economic downturns.

Looking ahead, it is paramount to underscore the value of continual learning and adaptation. The landscape of passive income generation is dynamic, influenced by technological advancements, market trends, and regulatory changes. As such, staying abreast of developments and being open to embracing new methodologies and investment vehicles will be pivotal in sustaining and expanding passive income streams. Moreover, fostering a proactive mindset geared towards identifying emerging opportunities and niche markets can unlock untapped potential for residual earnings.

Furthermore, as we chart the path forward, aspiring individuals should cultivate an entrepreneurial spirit rooted in innovation and creativity. Passive income ventures thrive on ingenuity and the ability to identify unmet needs or underserved demographics. Aspiring entrepreneurs should seize the opportunity to leverage their unique skills, expertise, and passions to carve out niche income channels that resonate with target audiences. Whether through digital platforms, real estate ventures, or intellectual property endeavors, harnessing creativity and originality can set the stage for enduring success.

In conclusion, the journey towards building passive income streams is a multifaceted endeavor that demands strategic foresight, risk management, continuous learning, and an entrepreneurial outlook. The insights garnered from our exploration provide a solid framework for individuals aspiring to forge their paths in the realm of residual income. By incorporating these learnings and embracing a proactive, innovative approach, readers are poised to navigate the evolving landscape of passive income generation with confidence and determination, ultimately paving the way towards sustainable financial prosperity.

Ways To Make Extra Income

The Power of Networking

Understanding the Essence of Networking

Networking is crucial for professional success and support. Building strategic relationships plays a fundamental role in career advancement, business growth, and personal development. By engaging with individuals across diverse industries and backgrounds, professionals gain access to a wealth of knowledge, opportunities, and resources. Moreover, networking fosters collaboration and fosters a supportive environment where expertise and experiences are shared for mutual benefit. Successful networking goes beyond simply exchanging business cards or digital contacts; it involves cultivating meaningful connections based on trust, respect, and shared goals. Understanding the essence of networking requires an appreciation for the value of each interaction, regardless of immediate returns. It is about investing in long-term relationships that contribute to both personal and professional growth. Networking provides exposure to different perspectives and opens doors to new possibilities, whether it's finding a mentor, exploring new career paths, or discovering potential partnerships. The essence of networking lies in proactively seeking out opportunities to connect with others, actively listening to their stories and experiences, and providing genuine support and assistance when possible. Ultimately, networking is about building a community of like-minded individuals who can offer encouragement, advice, and collaborative prospects. Recognizing the power of networking as a two-way street is essential; it entails contributing to the success of others as well as seeking support for one's own endeavors. Embracing authenticity and integrity in all networking efforts ensures that relationships are built on a solid foundation of trust and reciprocity. In essence, networking transcends transactional exchanges; it embodies the spirit of connection, empathy, and collective achievement. As individuals comprehend the profound impact of networking on their professional journeys, they can harness its potential to expand their horizons, achieve their aspirations, and make meaningful contributions to their respective fields.

Strategic Relationship Building

Building and maintaining strong professional relationships is a crucial component of success in today's interconnected business landscape. Strategic relationship building involves the deliberate cultivation of connections that can offer value, support, and opportunities for growth. It extends beyond simple networking to encompass the development of meaningful, mutually beneficial partnerships. At its core, strategic relationship building requires a proactive approach, genuine interest in others, and a focus on long-term collaboration. To lay the foundation for successful relationship building, individuals must first identify their objectives and target contacts who align with their goals. This process involves assessing the needs of one's own venture, as well as identifying potential collaborators or mentors who possess complementary skills, experiences, or resources. Once potential allies are identified, it is essential to prioritize outreach efforts effectively. Engaging with individuals through personalized and targeted communication demonstrates respect for their time and expertise and lays the groundwork for genuine connections. Leveraging existing connections and recommendations can also facilitate introductions and foster trust from the outset. As relationships begin to form, it is important to nurture them through regular and meaningful interactions. These interactions could take the form of informational interviews, collaborative projects, or mutual referrals. By consistently adding value to these relationships, individuals can build both credibility and goodwill, strengthening the foundation for future collaboration and support. Furthermore, strategic relationship building encourages active listening and empathetic understanding. Individuals must seek to understand the challenges, goals, and motivations of their peers, thereby demonstrating a genuine interest in their success. This depth of understanding forms the basis for meaningful engagement and establishes the groundwork for reciprocity in the relationship. Successful relationship building also entails accountability and reliability. Following through on commitments and proactively providing support when required fosters trust and demonstrates integrity. Finally, individuals must be prepared to adapt and evolve in response to feedback and fluctuations within the professional landscape. Flexibility and openness to new opportunities and perspectives solidify the capacity for sustained and impactful professional relationships. In conclusion, strategic relationship building is a fundamental skill set for achieving enduring success in any professional sphere. It requires intentionality, authenticity, and a commitment to ongoing cultivation. By prioritizing meaningful connections and actively nurturing those partnerships, individuals can lay the groundwork for lasting professional achievements.

Effective Communication Skills

Effective communication is the cornerstone of successful networking. It encompasses a range of verbal and non-verbal techniques that foster meaningful connections and lay the groundwork for mutually beneficial relationships. Strong communication skills are vital in articulating your ideas, expressing empathy, and building rapport with diverse individuals in various professional settings. To enhance your communication prowess, it is essential to cultivate active listening habits, demonstrate genuine interest in others' perspectives, and engage in clear, articulate dialogue. Effective communicators understand the power of body language and non-verbal cues, using them to convey confidence, understanding, and openness. They recognize the significance of verbal clarity, employing concise and impactful language to convey their message while avoiding ambiguity or misunderstanding. Additionally, mastering the art of asking insightful questions and offering constructive feedback can significantly enrich professional interactions, fostering trust and respect between networking partners. In today's digital age, the ability to communicate effectively extends beyond face-to-face interactions. The adept use of email etiquette, professional messaging platforms, and virtual meeting conduct plays a crucial role in cultivating lasting professional relationships. Furthermore, adapting one's communication style to suit different audiences and contexts demonstrates versatility and consideration, enabling seamless interaction with individuals from varied backgrounds and industries. To refine your written communication, attentiveness to tone, clarity, and professionalism are imperative in crafting correspondence that reflects your competence and reliability. Whether engaging in formal negotiations, casual conversations, or virtual exchanges, honing effective communication skills empowers professionals to navigate complex networking landscapes with confidence and finesse, ultimately propelling their careers forward.

Leveraging Social Media for Professional Growth

In today's digital age, the pervasive influence of social media cannot be overlooked when it comes to professional networking and growth. Social media platforms offer unparalleled opportunities for individuals to expand their reach, showcase their expertise, and connect with like-minded professionals. Leveraging social media for professional growth involves a strategic approach that integrates personal branding, content creation, and active engagement. Establishing a strong online presence begins with crafting a compelling personal brand that reflects your unique skills, values, and professional aspirations. By consistently sharing valuable insights, thought-provoking content, and success stories in your field, you can position yourself as an industry authority and cultivate a loyal following. Furthermore, engaging with industry peers, participating in relevant discussions, and offering genuine support can foster meaningful connections that may lead to promising collaborations or career opportunities. As social media facilitates global interactions, professionals can transcend geographical barriers and tap into diverse perspectives, ultimately broadening their knowledge and expanding their network. Additionally, staying updated on industry trends and advancements through curated social media content can enhance professional development and provide a competitive edge. It is important to maintain authenticity and professionalism in all interactions across social platforms, fostering trust and credibility within the professional community. Moreover, leveraging social media analytics and engagement metrics can provide invaluable insights into audience preferences and behavior, allowing for continuous optimization of content strategies and networking approaches. Lastly, integrating social media activities with offline networking efforts can amplify one's professional impact, creating a comprehensive and dynamic networking strategy. By thoughtfully utilizing social media as a tool for professional growth, individuals can harness its immense potential to establish meaningful connections, showcase expertise, and propel their careers toward greater success.

Networking Events: Maximizing Opportunities

Attending networking events provides a valuable platform for professionals to broaden their connections, exchange ideas, and cultivate meaningful partnerships. Whether it's a trade show, industry conference, or local meet-up, these gatherings offer unprecedented opportunities to interact with like-minded individuals and potential collaborators.

Building Mutually Beneficial Connections

Building mutually beneficial connections is a cornerstone of successful networking. In today's interconnected world, the value of establishing meaningful and reciprocal relationships cannot be overstated. The art of fostering such connections lies not only in identifying individuals who can assist us in our professional endeavors but also in understanding how we can reciprocate and provide value to them. At its core, this approach to networking is based on the principle of symbiotic reciprocity.

Mutually beneficial connections are founded on the idea that each party brings value to the relationship. This means taking the time to understand the needs and aspirations of those within your network and seeking opportunities to support them in achieving their goals. By prioritizing a genuine interest in the success of others, professionals can establish lasting and impactful relationships that extend beyond mere transactional exchanges. These connections thrive on authenticity, empathy, and a shared commitment to mutual advancement.

Forging mutually beneficial connections requires effective relationship management. This encompasses nurturing existing connections while also actively seeking new opportunities for collaboration and partnership. It involves proactively identifying ways to offer assistance, share knowledge, and provide support to those within your network. Furthermore, it necessitates the ability to recognize opportunities where your skills, experience, or resources can be instrumental in aiding others along their professional journey.

One crucial aspect of building mutually beneficial connections is the cultivation of trust. Trust forms the foundation of strong relationships and is cultivated through consistent, open, and transparent communication. Professionals must demonstrate reliability, integrity, and a genuine desire to contribute positively to the success of their network counterparts. By upholding these principles, professionals can engender trust and solidify their position as valuable and reliable partners within their network.

Elevating the concept of mutually beneficial connections transcends purely transactional networking practices. Rather, it fosters an environment of collaboration, support, and collective growth. It establishes a framework where professionals can leverage their diverse strengths and expertise to accelerate one another's advancement. Collectively, these connections contribute to a robust and dynamic professional ecosystem where success is celebrated as a shared achievement.

Ultimately, mastering the art of building mutually beneficial connections requires a genuine dedication to understanding, supporting, and uplifting others within the professional sphere. By embracing a mindset of reciprocity, empathy, and proactive engagement, professionals can harness the power of collective advancement, propelling both their own careers and those of their network counterparts to new heights.

The Role of Mentorship in Networking

Mentorship plays a pivotal role in the journey of professional networking, serving as a guiding force that shapes career trajectories and fosters personal growth. A mentor offers valuable insights, wisdom, and guidance based on their own experiences, paving the way for their mentees to navigate complex professional landscapes with confidence and clarity. The essence of mentorship lies in the transfer of knowledge, encouragement, and support, as seasoned professionals extend a helping hand to emerging talents.

One of the key benefits of mentorship in networking is the opportunity for mentees to learn from the successes and failures of their mentors. By leveraging these experiences, mentees can gain invaluable perspectives, avoiding potential pitfalls and embracing strategies that have proven effective. Furthermore, mentorship provides a platform for constructive feedback, enabling mentees to refine their skills and approach in a nurturing environment that prioritizes growth and development.

In addition to knowledge transfer, mentorship cultivates a sense of community and camaraderie within professional networks. Mentors act as advocates, empowering their mentees and creating pathways for them to access opportunities that may have otherwise been beyond reach. This advocacy not only facilitates professional advancement but also fosters an inclusive environment where diverse voices are heard and valued. Moreover, mentorship often extends beyond professional realms, encompassing personal development, work-life balance, and overall well-being.

Effective mentorship relationships are founded on trust, open communication, and mutual respect. Mentors serve as role models, embodying the qualities and ethos that they wish to impart to their mentees. As such, mentorship fosters a culture of continuous learning and excellence, driving the collective growth of professionals within a network. This collaborative approach reinforces the interconnectedness of individuals, emphasizing that success is not a solitary pursuit but rather a collective endeavor.

In today's fast-paced and dynamic professional landscape, mentorship serves as a linchpin in building resilient and adaptable networks. By investing in mentorship programs and cultivating meaningful mentor-mentee relationships, individuals and organizations can fortify their networks, ensuring longevity and relevance in an ever-evolving ecosystem. The role of mentorship in networking is not merely confined to individual development but extends to the enrichment of entire communities, creating a ripple effect of empowerment and progress. Embracing mentorship as an integral aspect of networking equips professionals with the tools, insights, and support needed to thrive in their respective fields, ultimately contributing to the collective prosperity of interconnected professional networks.

Creating Your Personal Brand

You have likely heard the phrase 'personal branding' thrown around quite a bit in recent years, and for good reason. In today's interconnected world, building and maintaining a strong personal brand is essential for professionals in any industry. Your personal brand is the unique combination of skills, experiences, and personality that you want to show the world. It is how you present yourself to others and how you are perceived.

Creating your personal brand starts with self-reflection. Consider your strengths, values, and goals. What sets you apart from others in your field? How do you want to be known and remembered? Once you have a clear understanding of your unique value proposition, you can begin to craft your brand identity. This includes elements such as your professional image, online presence, and communication style. It's essential to ensure that your personal brand is authentic and aligned with who you are. Authenticity is the key to building trust and credibility with your network.

Your online presence plays a significant role in shaping your personal brand. Ensure that your social media profiles, website, and professional platforms reflect the image you want to convey. Highlight your expertise, share valuable insights, and engage with your audience thoughtfully and respectfully. Consistency is crucial across all touchpoints – from your LinkedIn profile to your interactions at networking events.

Furthermore, effective storytelling can be a powerful tool in crafting your personal brand. Share your career journey, successes, and lessons learned in a compelling and relatable manner. Authentic stories can help humanize your brand and connect with your audience on a deeper level. Additionally, consider establishing yourself as a thought leader in your field by contributing to relevant industry publications, speaking at conferences, or hosting workshops. These activities not only enhance your credibility but also amplify your presence within your professional network.

Lastly, don't underestimate the power of networking in shaping and amplifying your personal brand. Building strong relationships with peers, mentors, and industry leaders can significantly influence how you are perceived professionally. Seek out opportunities to collaborate, mentor others, and add value to your network. Remember, your personal brand is an ongoing project that evolves with your experiences and accomplishments. Regularly review and refine your brand to ensure it accurately represents who you are and where you aspire to be.

Overcoming Networking Challenges

Networking is an essential aspect of career and business development, facilitating opportunities for personal growth, professional success, and the exchange of valuable resources. However, it is not uncommon for individuals to encounter challenges when engaging in networking activities. Overcoming these obstacles is critical to leveraging the full potential of networking. One common challenge is the fear of approaching new people and initiating conversations. Many individuals feel anxious or self-conscious in unfamiliar social settings, which can hinder their ability to connect with potential contacts. To overcome this challenge, it is important to adopt a positive and proactive mindset, focusing on the value that networking can bring and viewing each interaction as an opportunity for mutual benefit. Additionally, practicing and refining interpersonal communication skills can greatly alleviate this fear, making it easier to engage in meaningful conversations. Another hurdle in networking is the struggle to maintain authenticity while striving to make a strong impression. In a competitive environment, individuals may feel pressured to present a polished and idealized version of themselves, leading to a lack of genuine connection. Overcoming this challenge involves striking a balance between professionalism and authenticity. It is crucial to be genuine while also demonstrating expertise and competence in one's field. Sharing real experiences, challenges, and successes can foster deeper, more meaningful connections than superficial interactions. Finding common ground and being genuinely interested in others' stories can also help bridge the gap between initial impressions and lasting relationships. Moreover, navigating the diverse personalities and dynamics within networking environments can pose a significant challenge. Different individuals have varying communication styles, preferences, and expectations, making it challenging to establish rapport with everyone. Overcoming this obstacle requires adaptability, active listening, and empathy. By tuning in to others' verbal and nonverbal cues, individuals can tailor their approach to accommodate different personalities and build rapport effectively. Developing a nuanced understanding of social dynamics and being respectful of diverse perspectives can pave the way for fruitful connections. Additionally, overcoming networking challenges involves addressing fears of rejection and failure. The fear of being overlooked or dismissed can deter individuals from putting themselves out there and seizing opportunities. It is important to reframe rejection as a natural part of the networking process and a stepping stone to eventual success. Viewing each interaction as a chance to learn and grow, rather than a make-or-break opportunity, can greatly alleviate the fear of rejection. Finally, combating social insecurities and imposter syndrome is another prevalent challenge in networking. Individuals may doubt their qualifications or feel inferior compared to peers, inhibiting their confidence in networking situations. Overcoming this challenge involves recognizing one's own value, strengths, and unique contributions. Embracing a growth mindset and acknowledging that everyone has something valuable to offer can boost self-assurance and dispel feelings of inadequacy. Engaging in continuous self-improvement and seeking opportunities for personal and professional development can also reinforce confidence and combat imposter syndrome. In conclusion, networking challenges are inevitable, but they can be successfully navigated with the right mindset, skills, and strategies. Overcoming these obstacles empowers individuals to harness the transformative potential of networking, cultivate meaningful connections, and propel their career or business to new heights.

Sustaining and Nurturing Professional Relationships

In the realm of entrepreneurship and professional endeavors, the cultivation and maintenance of robust professional relationships are paramount to long-term success. Sustaining and nurturing these bonds not only fosters a sense of trust and reliability but also opens doors to new opportunities and collaborations. To achieve sustained professional relationships, individuals must prioritize consistent communication and engagement with their network. This encompasses active listening, expressing genuine interest in others' endeavors, and demonstrating reliability in fulfilling commitments. Furthermore, maintaining a high level of professionalism and integrity in all interactions solidifies one's reputation as a trustworthy and competent ally, thereby enhancing the potential for enduring partnerships. In addition to regular communication, it is crucial to recognize the importance of offering support and assistance to contacts within one's professional network. By providing valuable resources or guidance when feasible, individuals can showcase their commitment to mutual growth and success, reinforcing the foundation of their relationships. Moreover, acknowledging others' achievements and milestones through gestures like congratulatory messages or small tokens of appreciation goes a long way in affirming the value one places on their connections. Another key aspect of sustaining professional relationships involves leveraging networking events and platforms to continue fostering connections. Attending relevant industry gatherings, seminars, and workshops presents opportunities to engage with familiar contacts and expand one's network by establishing new associations. Proactive participation in such events demonstrates dedication and enthusiasm, thus contributing to the perpetuation and nourishment of professional ties. Furthermore, maintaining an active presence on professional networking platforms such as LinkedIn enables individuals to remain visible within their industry circle and reinforce their commitment to meaningful connections. Additionally, encouraging and facilitating connections among members of one's network also plays a pivotal role in sustaining and nurturing professional relationships. By acting as a connector and introducing mutually beneficial alliances, individuals demonstrate their commitment to seeing others thrive, thus cementing their role as an invaluable collaborator. Furthermore, providing endorsements or recommendations for colleagues and partners within one's network serves as a testament to one's confidence in their abilities, further fortifying the fabric of professional relationships. Ultimately, the sustained investment in nurturing professional relationships not only enriches one's career journey but also cultivates a sense of camaraderismo within the shared pursuit of success. Employing a dedicated approach to sustaining these bonds, characterized by consistent communication, support, proactive engagement, and facilitation of connections, paves the way for enduring and fruitful professional relationships that become indispensable assets in one's entrepreneurial voyage.

Ways To Make Extra Income

Maintaining Work-Life Balance

Introduction to Work-Life Balance

Work-life balance is crucial for long-term personal and professional success. In today's fast-paced and demanding world, finding harmony between one's career and personal life has become increasingly challenging. Striking the right balance between professional responsibilities and personal well-being is essential not only for individual health and happiness, but also for overall productivity and effectiveness in the workplace. Achieving work-life balance allows individuals to allocate time and energy to different aspects of their lives, including family, friends, hobbies, and self-care. It enables them to avoid burnout, reduce stress, and maintain a sense of fulfillment. Moreover, a balanced approach to work and life can lead to improved job satisfaction, increased creativity, and enhanced problem-solving abilities. When personal and professional boundaries are clearly defined, individuals can navigate their commitments more effectively. Recognizing the need to maintain this equilibrium is the first step towards cultivating a fulfilling and sustainable lifestyle. By establishing boundaries that safeguard personal time and well-being, individuals can enhance their overall quality of life and contribute positively to the organizations they are part of. Embracing work-life balance empowers individuals to excel in their professional roles while also tending to their personal needs, ambitions, and relationships.

Defining Personal and Professional Boundaries

Maintaining a healthy work-life balance is contingent upon one's ability to define and uphold personal and professional boundaries. In today's interconnected world, the line between personal and professional life can often become blurred, leading to increased stress and reduced overall well-being. By delineating clear boundaries, individuals can effectively manage their time and energy, minimizing the potential for burnout and enhancing both productivity and satisfaction. Personal boundaries encompass the limits one sets regarding personal space, time, emotions, and relationships. These boundaries serve as a safeguard for individual autonomy and self-care. Examples may include designating specific leisure time free from work-related interruptions, establishing communication norms with colleagues outside of working hours, and cultivating a home environment conducive to relaxation and rejuvenation. Conversely, professional boundaries pertain to the demarcation between one's personal life and work responsibilities. This involves setting expectations with employers or clients regarding availability, defining scope and limitations of work-related responsibilities, and fostering professional conduct in the workplace. By clearly defining these professional boundaries, individuals can reduce the likelihood of being consumed by work-related stressors and preserve critical personal time. It is essential to acknowledge that personal and professional boundaries are not static and may continually evolve based on individual circumstances and needs. With the proliferation of remote work and digital connectivity, individuals must adapt and recalibrate these boundaries to accommodate shifting work dynamics and personal commitments. One must also be cognizant of the impact of overstepping or neglecting these boundaries, as this can lead to feelings of resentment, anxiety, and diminished performance. Striking a harmonious balance between personal and professional boundaries necessitates open communication, self-awareness, and a willingness to advocate for one's well-being. As we delve deeper into the intricacies of work-life balance, it becomes apparent that the judicious establishment and preservation of personal and professional boundaries is integral to cultivating a fulfilling and sustainable lifestyle.

Prioritizing Tasks Effectively

Prioritizing tasks effectively is essential in achieving a healthy work-life balance. The ability to determine which tasks are most important and require immediate attention can significantly impact productivity and overall well-being. To begin, it is crucial to assess the urgency and importance of each task. This can be accomplished through methods such as the Eisenhower Matrix, which categorizes tasks based on their level of urgency and significance. By employing this framework, individuals can allocate their time and energy towards tasks that truly matter, rather than wasting resources on less critical activities. Furthermore, leveraging technology can streamline the prioritization process. Utilizing productivity tools and apps can aid in organizing and managing tasks efficiently, enabling individuals to focus on high-priority assignments. Additionally, establishing clear objectives for each task can provide a roadmap for success. By defining specific and achievable goals, individuals can ensure that their efforts are directed towards meaningful outcomes. It is also important to acknowledge the value of delegation. Identifying tasks that can be effectively assigned to others can alleviate workload and allow individuals to concentrate on tasks that align with their expertise and priorities. Moreover, setting realistic timelines for task completion is imperative. By creating a structured timeline, individuals can avoid feeling overwhelmed and prevent procrastination, ultimately leading to a more balanced approach to work and life. To prioritize tasks effectively, it is paramount to continuously evaluate and adjust one's approach. Reflecting on past experiences and learning from them can refine one's ability to assess and prioritize tasks. Additionally, seeking feedback from colleagues and mentors can provide valuable insights and improve prioritization skills. Lastly, maintaining a positive mindset and practicing self-compassion is vital. Balancing numerous responsibilities can often lead to stress and anxiety, making it essential to adopt self-care practices and seek support when necessary. In essence, prioritizing tasks effectively involves a combination of strategic planning, adaptability, and self-awareness. By honing this skill, individuals can enhance their efficiency, reduce stress, and foster a harmonious work-life balance.

Time Management Techniques

Time management is a critical aspect of maintaining work-life balance and achieving productivity. Effective time management techniques empower individuals to optimize their daily schedules, allocate resources efficiently, and minimize wasted time. One fundamental technique is the Eisenhower Matrix, a prioritization tool that categorizes tasks based on urgency and importance. By classifying tasks into four quadrants (urgent and important, important but not urgent, urgent but not important, neither urgent nor important), individuals can ascertain which activities to address first, delegate, schedule for later, or eliminate. Moreover, the Pomodoro Technique, a time management method developed by Francesco Cirillo, promotes focused work through intervals of concentrated effort (usually 25 minutes) followed by short breaks (5 minutes). This approach enhances concentration and combats mental fatigue, resulting in heightened productivity. Another valuable strategy is using SMART goals—specific, measurable, achievable, relevant, and time-bound—to set clear objectives and timelines. By establishing SMART goals, individuals gain clarity and structure, enabling them to effectively plan and allocate their time to achieve these targets. Furthermore, the Getting Things Done (GTD) methodology, popularized by David Allen, emphasizes the capture and organization of all tasks and ideas to facilitate efficient execution. By utilizing tools like to-do lists, calendars, and digital organizers, individuals can declutter their minds and focus on executing tasks, thereby increasing their overall productivity. Additionally, the 80/20 rule, also known as the Pareto Principle, suggests that 80% of results stem from 20% of efforts. Understanding this principle enables individuals to identify high-impact activities and prioritize them over less consequential tasks, leading to optimal time allocation and output. These time management techniques, when implemented effectively, enable individuals to navigate their professional and personal responsibilities with efficiency and effectiveness.

Leveraging Technology for Efficiency

In today's fast-paced and interconnected world, the role of technology in streamlining processes and optimizing efficiency cannot be overstated. From advanced project management tools to innovative communication platforms, leveraging technology is crucial for individuals seeking to maintain a healthy work-life balance. By utilizing cutting-edge applications, professionals can effectively manage their time, reduce manual workload, and achieve greater productivity. Incorporating digital calendars, task management apps, and automation software into daily routines can revolutionize how individuals approach their responsibilities. These tools not only aid in organizing various tasks but also enable better tracking and monitoring of progress, thereby facilitating a more structured workday. Additionally, integrating collaboration platforms and video conferencing solutions can vastly improve communication and teamwork, especially when working remotely. This seamless connectivity fosters efficient sharing of ideas and updates while mitigating the challenges of physical distance. Furthermore, the use of technology facilitates remote access to work-related data, allowing individuals to stay connected and productive from virtually anywhere. The integration of cloud-based storage and document management systems offers unparalleled accessibility and ensures that critical information is readily available. Moreover, artificial intelligence and smart algorithms have the potential to automate repetitive tasks, offering significant time savings and enabling professionals to focus on high-value activities. However, it is essential to exercise caution and maintain a healthy relationship with technology. Proactive management of digital tools is vital to prevent information overload and burnout. Establishing strict boundaries for technology usage and setting designated times for disengagement can help strike a balance between leveraging technology for efficiency and protecting personal well-being. Through thoughtful selection and utilization of technology, individuals can harness its power to enhance efficiency without compromising their overall work-life balance.

The Role of Mindfulness and Stress Reduction

In today's fast-paced world, it's easy to become overwhelmed by the constant demands of work and personal life. This chapter will explore the importance of mindfulness and stress reduction techniques in achieving a healthy work-life balance. Mindfulness involves being fully present in the moment, acknowledging thoughts and feelings without judgment, and cultivating a sense of tranquility. By practicing mindfulness, individuals can reduce stress and improve their overall well-being. One effective mindfulness technique is meditation, which allows individuals to focus on their breath, observe their thoughts, and cultivate a sense of calm amidst the chaos of daily life. Additionally, engaging in activities such as yoga or tai chi can help promote mindfulness and alleviate stress. It's important for individuals to make time for these practices, even if it's just a few minutes each day. Moreover, stress reduction goes hand in hand with mindfulness. Chronic stress can have a detrimental impact on both physical and mental health, leading to burnout and decreased productivity. Therefore, it's crucial to identify sources of stress and develop coping mechanisms. This may involve setting boundaries, delegating tasks, or seeking support from colleagues and loved ones. Furthermore, incorporating relaxation techniques like deep breathing exercises, progressive muscle relaxation, or visualization can help manage stress levels. By integrating mindfulness and stress reduction techniques into daily routines, individuals can enhance their ability to navigate challenges and maintain a healthy work-life balance. Cultivating a mindfulness practice and implementing stress reduction strategies not only benefit an individual's professional life but also contribute to their personal growth and overall well-being. In the upcoming section, we will delve into the critical aspect of balancing personal growth and career goals, exploring how individuals can align their aspirations with their professional endeavors while nurturing their holistic development.

Balancing Personal Growth and Career Goals

Achieving a harmonious equilibrium between personal development and professional aspirations is essential for leading a fulfilling life. Balancing the pursuit of personal growth with career objectives requires mindfulness, strategic planning, and adaptability. It is crucial to acknowledge that personal growth encompasses various dimensions, including intellectual, emotional, and spiritual enrichment. Simultaneously, aligning these personal aspirations with career goals creates a holistic approach to success. To navigate this multifaceted endeavor, individuals must first introspectively assess their core values, strengths, and areas for improvement. With this foundation, one can then integrate personal growth practices into professional development initiatives.

From a career perspective, setting specific, measurable, achievable, relevant, and time-bound (SMART) goals is imperative. These goals should be aligned with both short-term achievements and long-term aspirations, fostering a sense of direction and purpose. Concurrently, pursuing personal growth involves exploring new hobbies, acquiring knowledge through literature or courses, and embracing experiences that nurture individual well-being. Integrating these elements into a structured plan not only nurtures personal growth but also enhances professional performance, creativity, and overall satisfaction.

Maintaining a work-life balance is intrinsically linked to amalgamating personal growth with professional dynamics. This integration necessitates an understanding of potential conflicts, establishing clear boundaries, and embracing flexibility. Cultivating strong time management skills aids in prioritizing personal and professional endeavors without compromising quality or dedication. Furthermore, leveraging opportunities for self-improvement within the workplace, such as mentorship programs or skill enhancement workshops, consolidates personal growth alongside career advancements.

To realize this synergy effectively, communicating openly with colleagues and supervisors about personal development endeavors fosters an environment supportive of holistic growth. Additionally, actively seeking feedback and constructive criticism contributes to refining one's skills and propelling both personal and professional evolution. Embracing challenges with a growth-oriented mindset encourages continuous learning, resilience, and adaptability, thereby reinforcing the marriage of personal growth and career goals.

In essence, achieving balance between personal growth and career objectives demands ongoing introspection, proactive planning, and a commitment to holistic development. By nurturing personal aspirations while striving for professional excellence, individuals can cultivate a sense of fulfillment, purpose, and resilience in the pursuit of both personal and career-related ambitions.

Cultivating Healthy Relationships at Home and Work

Creating and maintaining healthy relationships, whether in the personal or professional realm, is essential for achieving a harmonious work-life balance. In today's fast-paced world, it can be all too easy to focus solely on career aspirations and professional success, inadvertently neglecting the crucial interpersonal connections that contribute to our overall well-being. Cultivating healthy relationships at both home and work requires dedication, empathy, and open communication.

At home, it's vital to prioritize quality time with loved ones while consciously fostering an environment of support, understanding, and love. This involves actively engaging in meaningful conversations, partaking in shared activities, and providing emotional support during both triumphs and challenges. Taking the time to truly connect with family members and friends not only nurtures personal bonds but also promotes a sense of belonging and fulfillment beyond one's professional endeavors.

Likewise, in the workplace, fostering healthy relationships with colleagues and superiors is instrumental in creating a positive and productive work environment. Effective collaboration, respectful communication, and offering support to peers are key components of cultivating a healthy professional network. Building strong relationships at work can enhance job satisfaction, boost team morale, and promote a more conducive atmosphere for creativity and innovation.

To cultivate healthy relationships both at home and work, individuals must foster effective conflict resolution skills, practice active listening, and demonstrate empathy and understanding towards others. Constructive feedback should be given and received with grace, always keeping in mind the mutual goals of growth and improvement. Moreover, maintaining a healthy work-life balance allows individuals to bring a positive and balanced energy to their relationships, ensuring that they can fully engage with and support their loved ones and colleagues.

Overall, investing time and effort into cultivating healthy relationships at home and work contributes significantly to an individual's overall happiness, productivity, and success. By nurturing these connections, individuals can navigate daily challenges with greater resilience, establish a support system for personal and professional growth, and foster a more fulfilling and contented life.

Recognizing Burnout: Signs and Solutions

Burnout is a critical issue that many individuals face, particularly as they strive to navigate demanding career commitments, personal responsibilities, and the pursuit of additional income streams. Recognizing the warning signs of burnout is essential for safeguarding one's mental and physical well-being. Common indicators of burnout include persistent feelings of exhaustion, detachment from work or personal activities, increased cynicism, and reduced productivity levels. It's crucial to acknowledge these symptoms and address them proactively.

One effective approach to combatting burnout is to create a supportive network and seek assistance from trusted colleagues, friends, or mental health professionals. Open dialogue and honest communication are central to overcoming burnout. Implementing stress-management strategies like mindfulness exercises, regular physical activity, and prioritizing self-care are pertinent in mitigating burnout triggers.

Additionally, defining and adhering to boundaries between work and personal life is pivotal in preventing burnout. This involves setting limits on work hours, practicing time management techniques, and taking designated breaks throughout the day. Individuals can also benefit from delegating tasks, saying 'no' when necessary, and creating buffer zones to focus on rejuvenation and relaxation.

Moreover, identifying the root causes of burnout is essential. This may involve reassessing career goals, evaluating work environments, and considering adjustments to daily routines. Engaging in self-reflection and recognizing the signs of burnout early on can facilitate timely intervention and prevent prolonged distress.

Furthermore, restoring balance through meaningful hobbies, creative outlets, and quality time spent with loved ones can counteract the effects of burnout. Embracing activities that bring joy, fulfillment, and relaxation outside of professional obligations is instrumental in replenishing emotional reserves.

Finally, holistic self-care practices, such as maintaining a balanced diet, getting sufficient rest, and seeking professional guidance when needed, are vital for combating burnout. By implementing proactive measures and fostering a supportive environment, individuals can regain equilibrium and develop resilience against the pervasive threat of burnout.

Crafting a Long-Term Strategy for Balance

Maintaining work-life balance is essential for long-term success and well-being. A sustainable approach to achieving balance involves crafting a strategic plan that encompasses various aspects of your personal and professional life. This section will delve into the key components of developing a long-term strategy for balance.

Setting Clear Goals and Priorities: Begin by defining your overarching goals for both your career and personal life. Clearly outlining your priorities will provide a roadmap for decision-making and resource allocation. Whether it's advancing in your profession, spending more quality time with family, or pursuing personal hobbies, having clarity on what matters most to you will guide your long-term strategy.

Creating Boundaries and Implementing Routines: Establishing boundaries between work and personal life is crucial for maintaining equilibrium. Consider implementing daily and weekly routines that factor in dedicated time for work, leisure, exercise, and relaxation. This separation fosters discipline and helps prevent work from encroaching on valuable personal time.

Investing in Self-Care and Well-Being: Prioritize self-care practices to nurture physical, mental, and emotional well-being. This may include regular exercise, meditation, hobbies, and time spent with loved ones. Additionally, seek opportunities for personal development and education to continuously enhance your skills and knowledge, contributing to overall contentment and fulfillment.

Leveraging Technology and Automation: Embrace technological tools and automation to streamline tasks and optimize efficiency. By reducing time spent on routine activities, you can allocate more energy to meaningful pursuits, thereby fostering a balanced lifestyle. From scheduling apps to smart home devices, harnessing technology can facilitate a smoother integration of work and personal commitments.

Regularly Assessing and Adjusting: Recognize that developing a long-term strategy for balance is an evolving process. Periodically evaluate the effectiveness of your approach and make necessary adjustments along the way. Life circumstances change, and staying adaptable ensures that your strategy remains aligned with your current priorities and aspirations.

Fostering Supportive Networks: Surround yourself with individuals who value and understand the importance of maintaining work-life balance. Seek mentorship, connect with like-minded professionals, and engage in communities that advocate for holistic well-being. Building a strong support system can offer guidance, encouragement, and perspective as you navigate the complexities of balancing competing demands.

By integrating these key elements into your long-term strategy, you can cultivate sustainable balance, enabling you to thrive both personally and professionally.

www.ingramcontent.com/pod-product-compliance
Lightning Source LLC
Chambersburg PA
CBHW071044240526
45471CB00014B/555